As a new-generation Nin scholar, Clara Oropeza expands Nin's mythic territory into a feminist realm of self-realization beyond the strictures of literal male autobiography and logocentric Modernism. Informed by the academic field of self-life writing, Oropeza provocatively reexamines the diary as an exploratory genre in which Nin "slants" fact into fiction largely through her creative role as a literary trickster. This is a daring, fresh interpretation of Anaïs Nin's artistic orientation.

—Suzanne Nalbantian, PhD; author of *Memory in Literature: From Rousseau to Neuroscience* (2003) and editor of *Anaïs Nin: Literary Perspectives* (1997)

Anaïs Nin: A Myth of Her Own is more than a groundbreaking study of a major modernist author, for this book reveals a mythic method to rival that of T. S. Eliot on Joyce, one superbly crafted by Nin to re-make being as feminine, creative, flexibly narrative, embodied and trickster-like. Oropeza traces a new direction in Modernist studies that is Jungian, feminist, ecocritical and liberatory. This superb book is a must for all serious students of Modernism, women writers, life writing, feminist theory and psychoanalytical approaches to literature, as well as scholars of interdisciplinary breakthroughs to a new paradigm in the humanities.

—Susan Rowland, PhD, author of *Jung as a Writer* (2005), *The Ecocritical Psyche* (2012) and *Remembering* Dionysus (2017)

Anaïs Nin

Anaïs Nin: A Myth of Her Own traces Nin's literary craft by following the intimacy of self-exploration and poetic expression attained in the details of the quotidian, transfigured into fiction. By digging into the mythic tropes that permeate both her literary diaries and fiction, this book demonstrates that Nin constructed a mythic method of her own, revealing the extensive possibilities of an opulent feminine psyche.

Clara Oropeza demonstrates that the literary diary, for Nin, is a genre that – with its traces of trickster archetype, among others – reveals a mercurial, yet particular understanding of an embodied and at times mystical experience of a writer. The cogent analysis of Nin's fiction alongside the posthumously published unexpurgated diaries, within the backdrop of emerging psychological theories, further illuminates Nin's contributions as an experimental and important modernist writer whose daring and poetic voice has not been fully appreciated. By extending research on diary writing and anchoring Nin's literary style within modernist traditions, this book contributes to the redefinition of what literary modernism was comprised, who participated and how it was defined.

Anaïs Nin: A Myth of Her Own is unique in its interdisciplinary expansion of literature, literary theory, mythological studies and depth psychology. By considering the ecocritical aspects of Nin's writing, this book forges a new paradigm for not only Nin's work, but for critical discussions of self-life writing as a valid epistemological and aesthetic form. This impressive work will be of great interest to academics and students of Jungian and post-Jungian studies, literary studies, cultural studies, mythological studies and women's studies.

Clara Oropeza is Professor of English Composition and Literature at Santa Barbara City College, California, U.S. Her research brings comparative mythology to literary studies and cultural theory. She is the author of several essays, most recently *The (Mal)Creation of Food the Monsanto Way: Returning a Mythic Sensitivity to Food Production.* She received her BA and MA in English Literature from California State University, Los Angeles and her PhD in Comparative Mythology and Literature from Pacifica Graduate Institute.

Anaïs Nin

A Myth of Her Own

Clara Oropeza

Routledge
Taylor & Francis Group
LONDON AND NEW YORK

First published 2019 by Routledge

2 Park Square, Milton Park, Abingdon, Oxfordshire OX14 4RN
52 Vanderbilt Avenue, New York, NY 10017

Routledge is an imprint of the Taylor & Francis Group, an informa business

First issued in paperback 2019

British Library Cataloguing-in-Publication Data
A catalogue record for this book is available from the British Library

Library of Congress Cataloging-in-Publication Data
A catalog record for this book has been requested
Names: Oropeza, Clara, 1970– author.
Title: Anaèis Nin : a myth of her own / Clara Oropeza.
Description: Abingdon, Oxon ; New York : Routledge, 2019. | Includes bibliographical references and index.
Identifiers: LCCN 2018019876 (print) | LCCN 2018019910 (ebook) | ISBN 9781315164885 (Master) | ISBN 9781351675482 (Web PDF) | ISBN 9781351675475 (ePub) | ISBN 9781351675468 (Mobipocket/Kindle) | ISBN 9781138057395 (hardback : alk. paper)
Subjects: LCSH: Nin, Anaèis, 1903–1977—Criticism and interpretation.
Classification: LCC PS3527.I865 (ebook) | LCC PS3527.I865 Z83 2019 (print) | DDC 818/.5209—dc23
LC record available at https://lccn.loc.gov/2018019876

ISBN: 978-1-138-05739-5 (hbk)
ISBN: 978-0-367-25266-3 (pbk)

Typeset in Times New Roman
by Apex CoVantage, LLC

Dedicación/Dedication

Para Mi Familia

And for the spirit of Anaïs Nin. May her words continue inspiring those setting out on the path that she so passionately paved.

Contents

With gratitude

I want to acknowledge Mark, my husband and co-conspirator in life, for always being my first reader and peerless editor. Thank you for always believing in me. I also thank you for assuring celebrations at the completion of each milestone at every stage in this process.

Thank you, Suzanne Nalbantian, for your attention to this manuscript and for your encouragement to publish this work. Your personal relationship with Nin contributed invaluable direction to my work. I thank Susan Rowland for being a supportive mentor and friend, and for always inspiring my own thinking; your support has been vital to this book.

While the writing of this book has been an act of dedication and passion for Nin's work, it has often seemed long, arduous and at times lonely. Hence, for their steady support throughout the writing of this book, my deep appreciation goes to my sisters and friends, *mi pistoleras*: Thelma Ruiz, Elvia Rodriguez, Hilda Shraddha Oropeza, Cris Oropeza, Luna Ruiz, Mercedes Taha, Chella Courington, April Heaslip, Carrie Hutchinson, Mona Ramirez and Nora Strejilevich. Thank you for your love and perpetual words of encouragement and for always nurturing me.

I also thank my students, whose appreciation and excitement for Nin's work continues to transform and energize me.

Finally, I want to recognize Emma Zunz for her canine support throughout this project. She has grounded my love for the non-human. I thank her for unconditional camaraderie and excuses to go for daily beach walks.

Permissions and acknowledgments

The epigraph featured in the Preface is taken from *Borderlands/La Frontera: The New Mestiza*. Copyright © 1987, 1999, 2007, 2012. Reprinted by permission of Aunt Lute Books. I thank you Joan Pinkvoss for permission to use this passage.

The passages I use as epigraphs in Chapters 1 and 2, were taken from *The Diary of Anaïs Nin*, Volume One (1931–1934), *The Diary of Anais Nin*, Volume Two (1934–1939) and *Incest: From a Journal of Love*. I thank Houghton Mifflin Harcourt Publishing Company for permission to use these passages.

Thank you to Harvard press for the permission to use Emily Dickinson's poem as an epigraph in Chapter 3. This poem is located in: *The Poems of Emily Dickinson*, edited by Thomas H. Johnson, Cambridge, Mass.: The Belknap Press of Harvard University Press, Copyright © 1951, 1955 by the President and Fellows of Harvard College. Copyright © renewed 1979, 1983 by the President and Fellows of Harvard College. Copyright © 1914, 1918, 1919, 1924, 1929, 1930, 1932, 1935, 1937, 1942, by Martha Dickinson Bianchi. Copyright © 1952, 1957, 1958, 1963, 1965, by Mary L. Hampson.

The original diary titles listed in Chapter 4 are taken from Anaïs Nin's archives housed in UCLA's Special Collections. I thank the Anaïs Nin Trust for giving me permission to use these original journal titles.

I thank Joan Didion and Chad Luibl, Janklow & Nesbit Associates, for permission to use an excerpt from Joan Didion, originally published in *The White Album*. Copyright © 1979. This passage is used as an epigraph in Chapter 5.

The epigraph included in Chapter 6 is taken from "Parable of Cervantes and the Quixote," copyright © 1998 by Maria Kodama; translation copyright © 1998 by Penguin Random House LLC; from *Collected Fictions: Volume 3* by Jorge Luis Borges, translated by Andrew Hurley. Used by permission of Viking Books, an imprint of Penguin Random House Publishing Group, a division of Penguin Random House LLC. All rights reserved.

An excerpt from Mina Loy's "Feminist Manifesto" is reprinted as an epigraph in Chapter 4. It is taken from *The Lost Lunar Baedeker: Poems of Mina Loy*. Copyright © 1996. Reprinted by permission of Roger Conover, literary executor of the Estate of Mina Loy.

I thank Hubert Zapf and Claire Weatherhead from Bloomsbury Publishing Plc. for permission to use an excerpt from "Literature as Cultural Ecology." Copyright © 2016. This is an epigraph in my Epilogue.

Preface

Tracing the faces of life, creativity and literature

> I want the freedom to carve and chisel my own face, to staunch the bleeding with ashes, to fashion my own gods out of my entrails. And if going home is denied me then I will have to stand and claim my space, making a new culture – *una cultura mestiza* – with my own lumber, my own bricks and mortar and my own feminist architecture.
>
> (Gloria Anzaldúa 1999)

My exploration of Anaïs Nin's (1903–1977) mythopoesis hopes to claim a space for the creative depth of a writer who ardently sought to give voice to the plurality of truths, as integral parts of her sense of self. Nin sought to fuse language with embodied experiences, including her personal visions of art, which she detailed in her diary for over 60 years. She kept a record of how language, intuition and the imagination both animates and informs the magnified, multifarious and deepened experience of the writer. It was her contention that narratives must be experienced through a triad pathway enmeshing the intellect, embodiment and imagination. This means that Nin's particular creed about the relationship between life and art is to be regarded under two distinct human needs: "one is a human need to be intimate with experience" and "then there's a second need in human nature which is to create something that has more permanence, which is the myth of our lives, the symbolic, spiritual significance of our lives" (*A Woman Speaks* 190).

Embracing the personal through self-investigation, as well as creating art containing the myth that holds the archetypal and spiritual, was Nin's way of critiquing the literary modes then in vogue that put emphasis on objectivity. For Nin, converging subjective experiences into art, including the profound, highly complex truths existing in multiple realms, remained an enduring interest throughout her life.

Nin ardently believed there was a way to write oneself out of the oppressive roles society imposed on a person. Women were not to reveal that they had a mind of their own, let alone uncover the multiplicity of voices and tensions in the domain of letters. For women, developing an appropriate authorial voice meant they had to cleverly overcome more than just societal disapproval; they had to defeat their own internalized socialization that posited writing was a masculine privilege. In subtle and not-so-subtle ways, often in terror, women risked their unguarded hearts. This means that to be a writer required the transformation of paradoxical and complex emotions. Nin reflects: "In the diary I can keep track of the two faces of reality. I have a record, I can balance one vision against another. As I write, I can dissipate the fear of alteration and loss . . . [the world] is born of intuition, of feeling. The transformation required of creation terrifies me. Change, to me, represents tragedy, loss, insanity" (2:111). Nin belongs to a lineage of women whose stories record the imbalanced past and whose pens fight against the falsehoods of identity.

Breaking conventions of her era by choosing to reject monogamy and live a child-free life, Nin was an anomaly. In addition, she defended the right for women to have the freedom of as many relationships as men had been privileged to engage in for centuries. Refusing to act under the sexist culture and literary influences of her time, Nin broke from gender constructs by writing about topics that were previously forbidden to women. Some themes in her work include homoeroticism and the exploration of women's sexuality. Also, metaphors of incest factor heavily in her early writing. As a diarist, engaging a literary genre that blurs the boundaries between truth and fiction, private and public, Nin strove to contend with the head/heart schism of literature. She also wrote fiction that is often difficult to categorize, and is frequently misread as merely self-inflating her own life. More accurately, in her fiction, Nin cobbles together a mythic method, including experimentation with language, and mythic tropes, from a hermeneutics of her own. The mythic tropes in her work testify to tensions that often combine experimental sensuality and physicality on one hand, and a deep desire to transform, create and transcend on another. Moreover, studying Nin's work reminds us that the relationship between the author's life, cultural milieu and work is never straightforward – nor should it be. By knowing that life does not explain the entire work, nor does the work explain the life, readers should remain curious and cautious when looking at the myriad ways in which life and art intersect.

Throughout her life Nin was enveloped in a cosmopolitan world of literature, art, music, dance and friendships from all walks of life. In the early 1930s, she published her first book, *D. H. Lawrence: An Unprofessional Study*, gaining her first public recognition as a writer. At the time, Lawrence's books were banned in the United States and causing scandal throughout Europe. Writing about a literary figure who in many circles was labelled a sexual crusader reveals Nin's pioneering spirit that would infuse her works for the rest of her life. In the late 1930s, Nin began publishing her novellas and short stories. As for the diaries, while they begin in 1914, Volume One (of seven), was not published until 1966. In the later 1960s and 1970s, feminist critics celebrated Nin's lyric prose and fresh subject position. It was a poetic voice about selfhood that many women yearned to hear. However, in the 1980s and 1990s, much of the feminist attention on Nin's literary achievements became exceedingly critical. Her language of feminine embodiment was seen as essentializing the feminine experience. Then the unexpurgated versions of Nin's *Diaries*, edited and published posthumously in the late 1980s and early 1990s, resulted in much sensationalizing by critics, casting a dark shadow on her literary accomplishments. Critics grew fixated with the drama of Nin's life and dismissed her as merely a confessional writer. Even then, some questioned her capacity for truth-telling. By using truth as the main criteria for close reading, some critics at the time accused Nin of fabricating stories, and others dismissed her works as containing merely autobiographical parallels with little to no artistic value.

As I read through some critics' responses to her posthumously published work, I am reminded of how often we hold women to higher, and often double, standards than we do men. We are more forgiving of male writers than of female writers. For Nin, a life of paradoxes often results in shaming and dismissal of her literary opus. I cannot help but wonder, how often is the life of a male writer bonded to events detailing scandal? Henry Miller's literary achievements are not relegated to his years of womanizing. The works F. Scott Fitzgerald wrote during the later years of his life, reflecting on the paradoxes that plagued him, were praised by critics as offering insights into the complexity of the writer at the center of the craft. In contrast, female writers do not seem to occasion the same sympathy and admiration. This context of sexism still animates borders and gender constructs today.

Nin in the 21st century

The wasteland that prevailed during Nin's time involved a disembodied culture that, while prizing wealth and power, was systemically engineered against women. Nowadays, while women in many parts of the world lead resistance, have more sexual and political freedom, and have the right to choose how they live their lives, sexism, sexist exploitation and oppression within patriarchy still needs to be challenged. The fight to build an equitable society is tied to the struggle of an inability to fully see populations based on gender and race. In some parts of the globe, girls do not control their own bodies, receive no education and struggle to have a voice and their lives be their own. Gender constructs continue to define our identities around the world in various ways.

Throughout the writing of this book, I was unfailingly moved by how deeply relevant still is Nin's ardent quest to realize a voice and to know its polyphonic nature, against androcentric ideologies. In 2016 in the United States there remained a vast uncertainty as to whether a woman had what it took to be president, largely based on her gender. We were told that when women are allowed into politics, they are not permitted to admit to having a separate private and public self. During this same presidential campaign, we were also reminded just how intently sexist politics dominate women's rights. The year I began this book, the largest mass demonstration in American history was organized by women. The Women's March in 2017 was attended by roughly three to five million people in around six hundred cities to advocate for women's rights and to voice intersectional concerns, following the election of Donald Trump as president of the United States.

While we continue to advocate for an equitable world for all, essential questions of our time are: what images feed our imagination as we desperately need to knit a critical understanding of the harmful structures that surround us? What are the narratives that we tell ourselves in hopes of harmonizing a sense of self, community and who we are in relationship to the earth? Who is willing to engage in this type of self-reflection required to tend to our communities? Nin offers a philosophical justification for why the cultivation of an interior world is essential to address calamities in society: not merely to resist alienation from oneself, but to better bridge our knowledge of others. Nin's feminism brings us a vision that is a necessary truth today: we must foster and affirm life as we oppose domination.

It is my hope that the close reading I offer of Nin's work will encourage a new generation to better recognize not only Nin's willingness to embrace the depths, mystery and fluidity of the creative process, but also to better appreciate the mythic method that she dedicated a lifetime to creating. For we in the 21st century must continue to find epistemological and aesthetic forms to deepen our understanding of ourselves, which in Gloria Anzaldúa's words ensues as an act of the "freedom to carve and chisel" our own expressions in a culture that must honor a plurality of feminine voices. From her subject position, Nin offers us clues about how to deepen our understanding of archetypal experiences in our own lives, the lives of others, and inspires us to live and write from a mythopoetic stance of one's own.

Works cited

Anzaldua, Gloria. *Borderlands/La Frontera: The New Mestiza*. San Francisco: Aunt Lute Books. 1999. Print.

Hinz, Evelyn J. Ed. *A Woman Speaks: The Lectures, Seminars, and Interviews of Anaïs Nin*. Chicago: Swallow Press. 1975. Print.

Nin, Anaïs. *The Diary of Anaïs Nin Volume Two (1934–1939)*. New York: Harvest. 1969. Print.

Chapter 1

Anaïs Nin

Self-life writing, myth and literature

Introduction

> She is the mermaid with her fish-tail dipped in the unconscious. Her creation will be to make articulate this obscure world which dominates man, which he denies being dominated by, but which asserts its domination in destructive proofs of its presence, madness.
>
> (Anais Nin 1937)

Writer and diarist Anaïs Nin (1903–1977), born in Paris to a French-Cuban-Danish mother and a Cuban father, believed that the intimate connection to one's subjective subtle and intricate developments, if well-tended, could guide the way to the convergence with the rest of humanity. As Nin writes, "the theme of the diary is always the personal, but it does not mean only a personal story. . . . The personal, if it is deep enough, becomes universal, mythical, symbolic" (3:153). Nin echoes not only the then-emerging field of psychology, but also alludes to cherishing the irresolvable voices that speak to the plurality of truths evading a single identity, which her literary works keenly examine. Nin's diaries are a "playground of subjectivities" where self and myth meander, and where death of one aspect of the self births another (Podnieks 66). In this way Nin, the diarist, engages in nature's truest cycle: life, death and rebirth. Nin quotes literary critic Leon Edel in his claim that "the Diary was nothing but a narcissus pool." To which Nin replied, "I have never seen a narcissus pool in which a thousand characters appeared at the same time" (*A Woman Speaks* 156). By referencing the medium of her diary as a many-voiced theatre where "a thousand characters" perform, Nin's overemphasis is on the creative process of interlocking an ontology of self, including mystery and fantasy, as recorded in both her diary and fiction.

The diary offered Nin the freedom that an artist seeks to discover the polyphony of voices that literature, in turn, explores, as seen in her fiction. In her essay "Speaking in Tongues," Zadie Smith draws our attention to the arduous progression of acquiring the many voices of self in both art and life. In reflecting on the worlds that both language and identity set forth, including the voices we "pick up along the way," Smith reminds us that in literary communities, the artist has been valued for having the flexibility required to speak in various "tongues" (133). To illustrate the pivotal point that literature has the capacity to "speak simultaneous truths," she quotes Keats on the gift of Shakespeare's creativity:

> At once it struck me, what quality went to form a Man of Achievement especially in Literature and which Shakespeare possessed so enormously . . . that is when man is capable of being in uncertainties, Mysteries, doubts, without any irritable reaching, after fact and reason.
>
> (Smith 134)

Nin's diarist and novelist credos value a polyphony of voices often irresolvable – and speak to a plurality of truths and experiences, often against a mythic backdrop. These characteristics are suited for more than the psychological and literary potentials of her art. They speak to Nin's perpetual interest in the convergence of art and life as narrative; she began writing in a diary at age 11, and continued until almost the end of her life, at age 73. Nin describes how her initial resolve to write a diary was the synthesis of disparate situations: "it was the way I was going to rebuild the bridge that was broken by the separation of my parents and by the uprooting to a foreign country" (*A Woman Speaks* 157). The diary, for Nin, held the "inner journey" that aspiring towards life and art demands. It was a place where "fictionalizing" was "helping the uprooting. To look at it as an adventure was the answer" (*A Woman Speaks* 223). The "fictionalizing" of a sense of the multiplicity of self is a concept this book thus examines.

This book proposes an analysis of the mythopoesis, the making of myths, by using Nin's diaries, fiction and theory as a conduit, in the works of a female writer. I submit that one should not simply define Nin's work as an attempt to codify an exclusive female aesthetic, or to portray a female artist who successfully integrates her art and her life. Rather, I argue that the continual process of the remaking of a personal myth, the subjective, symbolic and imaginative stories that construct her personal history, may be more fruitful than any single appropriate, authentic achievement.

Early in this book, my analysis explores Nin's work, specifically the *prima materia* in her diaries, and is initially contextualized within C. G. Jung's notion that the inner experiences pave the path towards becoming conscious of one's psychic process, contributing to self-realization. Jung used the term "personal myth" to suggest that his own personal history of the self-realization of his unconscious was told as a myth, thus indicating a more-than-individual context for meaning. Contextualizing Nin's early works within the conceptual framework of the Jungian paradigm seems to be an organic starting point, for Nin, though younger, was Jung's contemporary and shared some similar views. For example, just as Nin understood that "the personal life, deeply lived, takes you beyond the personal," C. G. Jung assumed that "true art resides in the fact that it has escaped from the limitations of the personal and soared beyond the concerns of the creator" (Jung 71). As a contemporary to Jung, she was also well-engrossed in the budding theories on psychic development, including sexuality, trauma and the life of the artist in the 1920s and 1930s. Importantly, Nin's emphasis on gender construction in personal myth may parallel the role of male subjectivity in that of Jung's work. Yet Nin's work does not contain the same authoritative tone or structure of a grand theory in her work.[1] For it was never Nin's intention, or style, to be objective. Also, one significant distinction between Jung and Nin lies in the scope of time spent probing the inner-self. Nin's diaries span from 1914 to 1974, 60 years. This makes Nin's diaries an important example of the depth and range of self-exploration, perhaps more so than in previous writers. In contrast, Jung's *Red Book*, while not structured as a diary, records 15 years of his life, from 1915 to 1930.[2] Moreover, this book does not seek to simply provide a parallel analysis of Nin's and Jung's personal myths; rather, a central question is, what does a close reading of Nin's work reveal about the epistemological and aesthetic methods that comprise a sense of self of a writer?

About this book

The questions raised in *Anaïs Nin: A Myth of Her Own* focus on Nin's mythic structure not only as a mode of inquiry, but as poetics of self-construction. Nin includes the personal, the textual, cultural, political and social in a space for the polyphonic sense of self to be created and re-created. In my study, I consider the expurgated editions of Nin's diaries, Volumes One through Seven (1931–1974), and Nin's unexpurgated posthumously published diaries, specifically, *The Early Diaries Volume Four* (1927–1931) and *Incest: From a Journal of Love* (1932–1934). Also, by closely reading Nin's novelettes *House of Incest*, *Winter of Artifice* and *Seduction of the Minotaur*, including the critical perspective of a New Historicist,[3] I trace the ways in which Nin, the weaver of myth, created a mythic method of her own.

In Chapter 2, I situate Nin as a late Modernist writer; from a historical perspective, Modernism characterizes the life and literature of Europe and the Americas in the era roughly between 1914 and 1940. I include a feminist approach to Modernism, which demonstrates that regardless of the claims to impersonality and universality, Modernism as defined by the conventional literary canon encrypts a white, male, heterosexual perspective. This book shows how Nin inevitably worked within male myths and plot structures constructed for the Modernist female artist while creating her own voice and method. By considering the diaries as a "playground of subjectivities" where personal myth is tended and a literary text is shaped, we could better understand how aesthetics of self-construction in an imagined private space, and at times performed, is nonetheless made public through the mediation of language. An analysis of Nin's mythopoetic method should not be equated with a mythologizing of Nin the historical figure. Rather, it is my hope that this mythic paradigm will expand the ontological possibilities from which to value Nin's literary oeuvre, the cultural milieu in which she wrote, and the embodied woman who created them.

Nin imagined that the female artist has access to two metaphorical worlds at once: the conscious and the unconscious, as "the mermaid with her fish-tail dipped in the unconscious" (2:235–236). Chapter 2 will further analyze the two symbolic worlds Nin references from the perspectives of sky-father and earth-mother consciousness, as first proposed by Baring and Cashford in *The Myth of the Goddess: Evolution of an Image*. Sky-father consciousness values logos, and abstract knowledge. In contrast, earth-mother consciousness values myths and relates to "the moral order of the goddess culture, inherited from the Neolithic." Earth-mother consciousness is "based on the principle of the relationship of the manifest to the unmanifest" (Baring, Cashford 159).

I examine the folktale of Scheherazade from *Arabian Nights* and the Sumerian myth "Inanna and the God of Wisdom," and show how these characters rely on their cunning and intelligence through the use of trickery and storytelling, as an example of archetypal characteristics that relate to the myth of the diarist. Chapter 3 demonstrates how fitting this mythic perspective is to understanding deeper meaning of the literary diary. My analysis illustrates that the myth of the trickster/trickstar as an archetypal phenomenon provides a clearer understanding of the polyvocal texture of Nin's diary, as well as the ways in which the diarist includes an inherent earth-mother consciousness to construct a sense of self.

In 1992 Nin's unexpurgated diaries, written in 1933–1934, were posthumously published under the title *Incest: From a Journal of Love*. Chapter 4 will contextualize these diaries within the emerging theories in the field of psychoanalysis, and Nin's tumultuous relationship with her father. It is within this context that I also analyze Nin's preoccupation with an incest metaphor in *House of Incest*, written between 1930 and 1933. The 1920s and 1930s were years between wars ravaging Europe, and paralleling critical decades in which Nin worked on crafting a literary style encompassing resultant paradoxes of terror, beauty, love and destruction. Also, as I offer my conjecture as to Nin's motivation for the posthumous publications of her diaries, I consider Nin's own responses to queries involving the editing process of the diaries, as noted in interviews given toward the latter years of her life.

Chapter 5 extends the historical and cultural context established in Chapter 4, by further exploring the intersection of Nin's diarist and novelist credos. Here I investigate Nin's creative process, including the incest metaphor, which is initiated in *House of Incest*, as it transmogrifies from the posthumously published diaries (1933–1934) into the short story *Winter of Artifice*. I propose that rather than allowing Nin's posthumously published diaries to be the last word buried in scandal, *Incest: From A Journal of Love* should be considered within a greater scope of Nin's creative process, and the historical, cultural and literary time period in which they were written, along with intricacies, which I point to, in the final handling of them.

Chapter 6 evaluates Nin's novelette *Seduction of the Minotaur* as Nin's feminist re-visioning of the ancient minotaur myth. I begin by outlining the literary interests in the minotaur myth prevalent in the backdrop of Nin's own novel.

By making Ariadne the protagonist, who is associated with the mazes and labyrinths in the myth of the minotaur, Nin captures protagonist Lillian's capacity to embrace her inner landscape as a feminine-embodied and spiritual journey. My analysis shows Nin's ontological understanding of recovering the embodied feminine psyche to suggest that biological bodies do indeed reflect psychic influence.

Anaïs Nin: A Myth of Her Own concludes by considering a recent example of mankind's lost sense of reciprocity with nature, as is evidenced in the developing relationship between the industrialization of food and patenting elements of nature. Here I propose that, as we learn to better live on this planet, diary writing has an eco-minded aspect that may contribute to changing human treatment of non-human nature. I demonstrate that Nin's diaries are a model of exploring the link between language, inner ecologies and self-disclosure, which invites us – often compels us – to take new risks as we reflect on our mythologies. An eco-minded diary can be used as a tool for community building by risking the personal, not merely as an ego-driven effort, but through sensibilities including mythic tropes that link art and life. It is in this way that Nin's work demonstrates a relationship between myth, life and literature that contrasts with other Modernist mythic methods.

Scholarship and the vector of the literary diary

Anaïs Nin's diaries unveil the process of constructing self, and highlight the relationship between life, myth and narrative. To better understand Nin's contributions to diaries as a literary genre, as well as the theoretical framework I'm proposing through which to understand diaries, including the myth of the diarist, it is first necessary to situate the theoretical definitions of autobiography and to understand when and how diaries enter this debate. This literary and historical context reveals both what autobiographical critics have valued, and how they have defined what constitutes self through the mediation of language. While theoretical definitions of autobiography, constructed by white, male critics, exclude the specific mention of diaries, feminist scholars have challenged those early definitions. I am interested in charting this shift. Prior to the 1970s, women's autobiographical writings were trivialized as a purely confessional mode of writing, not complex enough to warrant literary criticism. The double bind of treating women's self-life writing as merely confessional, and holding them to different standards than self-life writings authored by male writers, particularly in the genres of autobiography and memoir, persisted well in to the 1990s. It is then necessary to first examine general autobiography scholarship, before proceeding to specific scholarship about the diary as a literary and historical context for my own entry into the construction of Nin's mythopoesis.

While women have been writing and contributing to the literary canon for decades, in the 1960s and 1970s, theories of autobiographies continued to dismiss, exclude and misidentify women's self-life writings. An early seminal essay defining autobiographical writing is "A Theory of Autobiography," published in

1972, by James Olney. According to Olney, autobiography is the place where man sets forth his uniquely creative impulse precisely because autobiography is "an attempt to describe a lifework . . . a man's autobiography is thus like a magnifying lens, forcing and intensifying that same peculiar creative vitality that informs all his collected works" (4). Olney argues that the meaning-making process, for each autobiographical writer, is exclusive to his selected metaphors. That is, it is only through metaphors that meaning is constructed. He defines metaphor as "something known and of our making, or at least of our choosing, that we put to stand for, and so to help us understand, something unknown and not of our making" (30). The importance of Olney's contribution to the definition of autobiography is that he posits that metaphor is essentially a way of knowing. By revealing the process in which the psyche realizes itself through metaphor, Olney is also suggesting the link between myth and autobiography, for myth is also a way for the psyche to experience the self metaphorically. Also, the autobiographer, as is true for the diarist, will use the myths central to their being in order to further depict the uniqueness of their subject position.

In a later essay dated 1980, "Autobiography and the Cultural Moment: A Thematic, Historical and Bibliographical Introduction," Olney argues that "the act of autobiography is at once a discovery, a creation, and an imitation of the self" (4). Olney raises questions about identity, creation (as through fiction), and myth in autobiography. He reveals the possibility of broadening the definition of autobiography to include "creation," "discovery" and fiction. Yet in this essay, he excludes the possibility of other forms of autobiography, such as the diary.

In his essay "Conditions and Limits of Autobiography" (published in 1980, originally dated 1956), George Gusdorf posits that the goal of the autobiographer is to reach a conscious understanding of himself. He understands an autobiography as "one of the means to self-knowledge, thanks to the fact that it recomposes and interprets a life in its totality" (38). The notion that an autobiography can hold the totality of a life story does not take into account one of the most fascinating qualities of self-life writing: the ability to which "totality" and "self" might coincide neither in consciousness nor in language. Gusdorf's definition also does not encompass the forms of self-life writing that include the creative unconscious, and those that are not intended to create a cohesive sense of self over time. Gusdorf adds, "each of us tends to think of himself as the center of a living space" (29). The emphasis is thus placed on the "I" as a singularity of importance, for according to Gusdorf, "he is not engaged in an objective and disinterested pursuit but in a work of personal justification" (39). Gusdorf's constricting definition of self-life writing raises issues of self-construction and restricts the motivation of the author's self-importance as a form of mortality. These issues are challenged and re-visioned by feminist scholars such as Domna C. Stanton, Shari Benstock and others. This means that while Gusdorf and Olney limit their focus to the lives of great men such as Augustine, Rousseau and Goethe, whose lives and works assumed their importance as cultural capital, feminist scholars expand the definition to include diaries and other forms of self-life writing that include a polyvocal sense of identity, as well as multiple discourses in which women can write.

What emerges from the early theoretical trajectory, as noted above, is evidence that the study of autobiography is justified on the grounds that the genre has a canon that excludes women and men from marginal groups, and a history of valuing the humanist idea of the unique individual moving to locate a unified self. Moreover, in the 1980s, a new body of feminist scholarship was launched in efforts to define women's autobiographies, away from gender essentialist notions. A recurring critical issue for many writers and critics is thus; how to define women's writings without falling into gender essentialism, while still emphasizing that women writers recognize the importance of aesthetic standards, both in their own work and in evaluating that of others.

Importantly, the ensuing decades have brought a shift in the status of autobiography, as feminist scholars of autobiography have re-visioned this definition by looking at the hegemonic discourse – that is, the language of power – that created early autobiography scholarship. To debunk the mainstream definition of autobiography, and to study women's autobiographical practices, feminist scholar Domna C. Stanton proposes the nomenclature "autogynography" to comprise women's autobiography. Stanton edits *The Female Autography* (1984), and in the opening essay of this collection "Autogynography: Is the Subject Different?" Stanton frames her argument parallel to Virginia Woolf's narrator in *A Room of One's Own*. Stanton sees women's life writings, existing at the margins of the literary world, as symbolic of an order that places women in a lower status than men. In this way, she examines the interrelations between the problematic of women's place in society and their impulses towards, and modes of, self-life writing. She argues that different from a "phallocentric system," the privileging of rationality deemed as masculine, "the *graphing* of the *auto*" was an act of self-assertion that denied and reversed woman's status. To this assertion, Stanton adds that autogynography has a global and "essential therapeutic purpose: to constitute the female subject" (15). Yet despite the aim of self-assertion, the construction of a self is problematized because of women's symbolic status as marginal "other" in patriarchy. Stanton suggests a connection between women's subject position as a "different" standing in the symbolic order, and the notion that the diary is a literary space where the diarist not only explores the conflicting roles within a patriarchal order, and the desire for a creative selfhood, as in Nin's case, but also informs the complex construction of a new mythology to live by. More importantly, by including the word "gyno," as in autogynography, Stanton's nomenclature itself writes the female body into the process of self-life writing, thereby inviting critical observations about the connection between writing and the body.

Stanton contributes the critical point that for women, there has been a deep cultural need to assert a subject position that for too long has been denied and marginalized by androcentric definitions of self-life writing. Her work further emphasizes an attitude of marginalization that the female writer internalizes, and which in many situations fuels the need to construct and assert the female subject position, a central theme in Nin's work. A pivotal tension in Nin's literary diaries deals with her effort to define experiences as feminine. Nin was keenly aware and concerned with the tension surrounding what it means to write from a woman's subject position. Yet for her, this concern meant not prescribing an aesthetic for women artists, but learning how to adapt and survive as a female writer. Her diaries provide insight to this creative tension, as I explore in this book.

Moreover, whereas Gusdorf credits the control of the autobiographical writer for its command of its content, Shari Benstock in "The Female Self Engendered: Autobiographical Writing and Theories of Selfhood" sees it as indicative of the overemphasis on authority (1999). Benstock points out that for Gusdorf, the subject is made an object of investigation, and where the gaps exist in the temporal and spatial dimension, so the texts are often successfully hidden from the reader and writer. This makes the narrative seem seamless, organic and overall validating to the understanding that autobiography is a result of the conscious control of artist over subject matter. This relates back to the belief that autobiography is the life history grounded in authority. To advance a critical discussion of autobiography beyond Gusdorf's definition, Benstock poses the critical question of the extent to which the "self" and "self image" might not coincide, or rather, can never coincide in language, as I noted earlier. She emphasizes instead that the process which the autobiographer takes to differentiate himself from others is language: a "symbolic system that both constructs and is constructed by the writing subject" (8). Therefore, one way to describe the notion that the male autobiographer keeps "I" at a greater distance than the female autobiographer, for Benstock, stems from the idea that "the female autobiographers are more aware of their 'otherness,' but our experience of its social and political effects comes under the terms of another law – that of gender" (8). Here Benstock's argument expounds on the concept that the subject position is an inherently engendered one; this debate has a long historical context that cannot be extricated from our reading of autobiographies, including diaries. It is crucial to recall this gender double bind in diaries and autobiographical writing that has been prevalent for too long. It has been to the immense disadvantage of women throughout history to be considered to have nothing to contribute to greater ways of knowing and being, which is indeed Benstock's point.

Scholars such as Sidonie Smith and Julia Watson, in *Women, Autobiography, Theory: A Reader* (1998) map the theoretical perspectives on subjectivity that have contributed to the redefinition of autobiography as a literary genre. Smith and Watson take into account the reasons for the growing interest in women's autobiography as well as the shift in perspectives on subjectivity re-formulation. In the 1960s and 1970s, the field of women's autobiographical studies stemmed from a growing academic interest connected to the growth of gender, ethnic and area studies programs interested in fulfilling a demand for texts that speak to diverse experiences from diverse subject positions (5). At the time (1960s and 1970s), women read autobiographies authored by women with a desire to deepen their own understanding of their life. It was the "mirroring" of a women's own unvoiced experiences and aspirations that drew most readers to autobiography, and this is the historical time period (1966) of the publications of Volume One of Anaïs Nin's early diaries. It was in the 1970s that feminist critics sought to recover "the long-out-of-print writings of women over centuries and framing them as a tradition rather than as 'marginal' or 'failed' efforts to write master narratives for male audiences" (Smith and Watson 6).

Importantly, it was through research done by feminist critics on writings of women that later shifted the interest in reading women's autobiographies from merely mirroring a women's experience, to a more analytical exploration of not only the lives of women, but their craft as writers. It is critical to point out that women writers were recognized not only for breaking the silence, but also for their contributions to aesthetic standards. The questioning of gender and race barriers that existed in the literary canon were critical interventions, as they helped rethink literary standards to move away from existing structures of domination. At this point, women could better understand that writing from a subject position of the personal, of having an agenda and political concern was a critical and worthwhile endeavor. As many of the feminist critics point out, the "personal" inspired many women to write, and their dedication to the craft of writing to expand.

Diary scholarship

The word diary has its roots in the Latin word *dies*, day, connecting the diary to the ritual of a daily embodied act of writing. Diaries, in the traditional sense, are private accounts of a person's life. Dating from the Heian era in Japan (794–1185), diaries were called pillow books, written by women and kept secret. In the West, however, diaries have been considered both personal and public. Contributing to the feminization of the diary was the implementation of the so-called "etiquette books," in the 1800s, "designed to instruct young women how to gauge and improve their feminine conduct through particular diary-keeping habits and techniques" (Podnieks 51). These etiquette books became a "feminized" site for upper- and middle-class women, linking diary writing with privilege, a link reflected in Nin's diary. This historical view traces women's modern experiences with an impulse towards a daily practice of writing a diary. Also, this diaristic history contributes brilliantly to the debate of reasons why works authored by women have been systematically and traditionally marginalized.

Moreover, Robert A. Fothergill in *Private Chronicles: A Study of English Diaries* (1974), stresses the literary value of the diary as he delivers a historical account of the evolving tradition of the English diary (14). The diary, Fothergill points out, does not have one originating source. Rather, "it is best regarded as the coalescence of a number of pre-diary habits into a form that exceeds its component elements" (14). The pre-diary habits are reflected in four types of diaries such as journals of travel, "public" journals, journals of conscience and journals of personal memorandum (14).

Consequently, Fothergill reminds us that the specific role that a diarist will accord to his or her diary varies. For many diarists who were also writing in other literary genres, a central function is that the diary serves as a hearth for creative fluidity. Such was the case for many literary women, such as Fanny Burney (1752–1840), Virginia Woolf (1882–1941), and Anaïs Nin (1903–1977). The diaries of these three women in particular break from the tradition of keeping the diary private. In 1788, at the age of 15, Burney began writing her diary with an idea that it was to be a place of emotional refuge. She playfully writes, "To have some account of my thoughts, manners, acquaintance and actions, when the hour arrives in which time is more nimble than memory, is the reason which induces me to keep a Journal. A Journal in which I must confess my every thought must open my whole heart!" (18). Burney wrote in her diary until 1840, and it became her major literary work, published in 1832. Beginning in 1915, Virginia Woolf kept a diary, and at the age of 22, she began to use the diary as a way to seriously explore its capacity as a literary form for its flexibility. In a diary entry dated October 23, 1917, Woolf reflects: "another lapse in this book, I must confess; but, if I do it against my humour I shall begin to loathe it; so the one chance of life it has is to submit to lapses uncomplainingly" (1:65). Woolf finds comfort in the diary's capacity to contain fluidity and spontaneity. Also, she comes to experience her diary as a place for liberation and ease. In a later entry of 1939, Woolf notes: "oh how gladly I reach for this free page for a 10 minute scamper after copying and re-copying, digging in these old extract books for quotes all the morning?" (3:244). Anaïs Nin, too at times, regards the diary as a means to envelop herself in freedom of expression and comfort: "I do not feel this tension when I am writing. I am at ease in the diary. When will creation and life fuse for me, and when will I be equally at ease in both?" (5:39). Later in her life, the purpose of her diary morphed into a life-holding vessel: "Life only became real when I wrote about it" (7:310). It was the flexibility of the genre that Nin praises: "At twenty it's different from thirty and at thirty it's different from at forty . . . this year it has become a correspondence with the world, and probably that is the right ending for a diary, that it would start as a river and then flow into an ocean" (*A Woman Speaks* 180). In its mercurial flexibility, the literary diary is a place to "get lost" and re-claim psychological and poetic insight.

From a mythic perspective, being called to the diary day after day evokes an image of Hestia, the first Olympian who is placed in the center of Greek life as the hearth. Through her glowing, warm coals, Hestia grounds the diarist in both a physical and psychological space to write oneself a home. In the Homeric hymn, Hestia protects and bestows humankind with good things. Hestia's myth is a reminder for the diarist as s/he collects a composite of myths seeking form and coherence, to not only entertain and warm up to ideas, but to value a psychic homecoming that inspires a place for creativity. James Hillman, in his essay "In: Hestia's Preposition," sees Hestia as one who "governs the inner psychic structure" (238). As the goddess of slow-burning yet smoldering coals, akin to contemplation, Hestia holds the power to bring the soul into a state of dwelling inside a hearth. The spatial metaphor that holds creativity evokes a sanctified space for the diarist to reside.

In her essay "Mimesis: The Dramatic Lineage of Auto/Biography" (1987), Evelyn J. Hinz emphasizes three dramatic characteristics in autobiography and the diary, such as elements of conflict and dialogue, a sense of performance and/or spectatorship and a mimetic or referential quality. Hinz links drama into the ancestry of self-life writing. By acknowledging these dramatic affinities, according to Hinz, we come to see drama as the "sister art" for autobiographies and diaries (209). Hinz, moreover, parallels the life of the actor as taking on another self with that of the autobiographer (200). Interestingly, she connects Nin as the "most famous twentieth-century diarist" with an aspiring stage performer. This is a topic that I delve into further in Chapter 3.

The link between diaries and the recurrent "patterns of experience" relate to the archetypal qualities, images from the unconscious that animate the individual and the collective, in the myth of the diarist that this book examines. Hinz values the dramatizing quality in self-life writing, as does Nin in her diaries. The affinities between self-life writing and drama, resonate with a depth psychological understanding of ritual, writing and performance. James Hillman writes, "the ritual of theater, of religion, of loving, and of play require concrete actions which are never only what they literally seem to be" (137). He reminds us that ritual motions have a way of psychologizing and of deliteralizing events as they are performed. A critical question I investigate is, what does a close reading of the archetypes in Nin's diaries from the hermeneutics of depth psychology reveal about myth, fantasy, performance and self-construction? I look at this specifically in Chapter 3.

Judy Simons's book *Diaries and Journals of Literary Women from Fanny Burney to Virginia Woolf* (1990), informs my work on Nin's diaries as a genre that allows women a subversive space for self-creation. Simons argues that despite the restricted forms of expression, women have, through their diaries, been able to break hegemonic conventions and provide decisive and coherent images of self (196). Her study of diarists includes Dorothy Wordsworth, Mary Shelley, Elizabeth Barrett Browning, Louisa May Alcott, Edith Wharton, Katherine Mansfield and Virginia Woolf. Simons's study poses such questions as, what relationship can be traced between personal writings and literary texts for publication by the same author? Do the diaries offer insight into the unique difficulties women might have faced in the production of literature? I will consider these questions specific to Nin's diaries and fiction later in this book.

An examination of the ongoing critical conversation regarding diary discourse and the academy can be found in *Gender and the Journal: Diaries and Academic Discourse* (1992), by Cinthia Gannett. The early part of her study looks at the various motivations for a diarist to write and how such motivations could relate to gender. Gannett argues that the difference in gender discourse "lies in that a woman's relationship to language remains paradoxical, as the word is simultaneously foreign and familiar" (47). Thus, in order to speak or write, women "must both/either accommodate to this alienation, and/or find alternative modes of expressions – ways to subvert the dominant discourse or move outside it" (48). Gannett posits that women have learned to speak through "fissures" and "gaps" in the discourse, writing or speaking from the most direct experience of their bodies in order to reconnect language, life and text (48). More importantly, Gannett's study extends to university classroom research to learn more about how the university defines and practices the journal. She argues that the diary, because of its association with women's experiences, voices and perspectives, has been labeled a problem, a Pandora's box (193). Journals were entering the universities in the 1960s and 1970s through the side door of Women's Studies, a technique called "personal-style pedagogy" (196). However, as a shift in the 1980s, process models of composition were critiqued for being based too much on discovery of an authentic voice or self, and for using an outdated approach to self and language. It is at this time that "mastery of academic writing had become once more an accepted goal of composition pedagogy" (196). Overall, Gannett's work discusses how both teaching diaries and using diaries are under attack, and she advocates for ways that we can change the prevailing modes of discourse that are still privileged in academia (198). Gannett's work outlines the importance of validating the diary as a valuable epistemological form to be both studied and practiced in the academy. We must encourage diaries to be considered and brought forth as an epistemological tradition to which women have been contributing for extensive periods of time, yet have been overshadowed by other, more masculine rhetorical modes of knowing.

Another ongoing critical conversation about women's diaries is reflected in Anna Jackson's *Diary Poetics: Form and Style in Writers' Diaries, 1915–1962* (2010). Jackson cautions that the dominance of the canon of autobiography by male writers has led to a false universalization of a masculine tradition (4). Throughout her book, Jackson notes that theorizing diary writing as expressions of femininity or as responses to women's social conditions is incorrect. In this study, Jackson analyzes the diaries of Joe Orton and John Cheever to show that they too reveal similar gaps and silences, as do the diaries of women writers (4). Jackson disagrees with diaries being read as mere facts of the diarist's life. Thus, Jackson's interest is in reading the literary effects of the diary, the literary and formal possibilities of the diary as a genre. Central to her focus on the diary is its "sequential nature," and how it is that over time, entries come to piece together a text with a larger significance. She calls this the autonomy of the entry, and the unifying effects of the sequence, she argues, can be seen as opposing forces. Jackson's work relates the diary to a literary work, pointing to the notion that the diary text itself may be constructed through different narrative inscriptions. As I shall show, the same is evident in Nin's exploration of identity in the diaries.

In *Daily Modernism: The Literary Diaries of Virginia Woolf, Antonia White, Elizabeth Smart, and Anaïs Nin* (2000), Elizabeth Podnieks traces the historical conditions of the diary that arguably solidifies the association of the diary to women. By the 19th century, the effects of the industrial revolution induced a split between the public and private spheres; the private sphere became synonymous with women (35). Meanwhile, the emergence of psychology as a discipline contributed to a redefinition of "self." Podnieks focuses on the diary as a significant literary space for women authors, and underscores that the diary is not an inherently female form, but rather a characteristic one. Still, according to Podnieks' research, women were among the first English diarists, and played a major role in the development of the genre, yet they are not given canonical credit. Lady Margaret Hoby's (1571–1633) diary is a Puritan spiritual and moral account that progresses into a record of daily thoughts. By diverging from the Puritan regimen expected of her in favor of a more personal and domestic recording, it signals that from the beginning women played a crucial role in the development of the genre (46). Yet it is the diaries of Samuel Pepys and James Boswell that are typically given credit for establishing the genre in its early form.

Podnieks thus seeks to answer the question, why are women not associated with the diary in the early canon? Why, then, have Samuel Pepys and James Boswell had canonical rights to founding and influencing the diaristic tradition, which has consequently been recognized as a largely female genre? (47) This trajectory is important to trace, as it reveals the ways in which women have been excluded as pivotal contributors to important literary traditions. One proposed answer to why the early study of diaries is attributed to male authors is the fact that Pepys, for instance, had the advantages of being a man, meaning that he had access to an education and to publishing, and had a public and political career. He left his diaries to his alma mater, Magdalene College, Cambridge to be studied (48). We are left to imagine how many diaries authored by women did not have access to the same privilege, leading to a lack of recognition in the overall canon of self-life writing.

In addition, Podnieks contextualizes the history of the rise of the diary as it happens parallel to the development of the novel. Not only does her work reveal a similar "othering" of writings authored by women, but it also draws on the diary as a literary genre with particularly Modernist literary qualities. The link between the Modernist novel and the diary is Podnieks' way of emphasizing the fictional aspects of self-representation in diaries. Comparing the concept of the "polyvocal aspect of diaries," Podnieks astutely observes that the diary is "illuminated as a playground of subjectivities" (66). Podnieks considers the diary as a "subversive" genre for women and analyzes how women use the diary form to disrupt a sexist Modernist movement. Drawing on her theory, I evaluate Nin's diaries as comprised of Modernist qualities and characteristics. My work looks at the diary as a "playground of subjectivities," where personal myth is constructed, and as also a "battlefield," where the death of one aspect of the self births another.

Diary as a literary genre

It is important to set forth a working definition of the literary diary. Let us consider Elizabeth Podnieks' definition:

> The diary is a book of days presented in chronological sequence, though not necessarily recorded as such. It inscribes the thoughts, feelings, and experiences

> of its author and may depict the social, historical, and intellectual period in which she or he lives and writes. Aspects of the author's character may be denied or repressed, or acknowledged and celebrated. The author is identical to the protagonist in this life story, though the author necessarily narrates it through varying layers of personae or invented, fictive selves. The diary is an open-ended book, but it may include internal closures and summations. By virtue of its status as a book of days, it is disconnected, yet it may offer structural and thematic patterns and connectives. Though likely written spontaneously, it is a consciously crafted text, such that the diarist often takes content and aesthetics into account. Finally, though composed in private, the diary is not necessarily a secret document. It may be intended for an audience: an individual, a small group of people, or a general public, and either contemporary with or future to the diarist's lifetime.
>
> (43)

The broad nature of this definition points to the flexibility as well as the genres capacity to contain both earth-mother and sky-father consciousness. This way we can better appreciate the diary's mythic yet complex nature. The diary, as are most genres, is linked to a set of literary conventions. Thus, due to its inherent ability to narrate a personal myth, we are reminded that craft through aesthetics is part of the production of the text. In her essay "I Write for Myself and Strangers: Private Diaries as Public Documents," Lynn Z. Bloom begins by citing a reference to Nin's omission of "divid[ing] her time between two husbands," as an example that "it is a mistake to think of diaries as a genre composed primarily of 'private writing,' even if they are – as in many women's diaries – a personal record of private thoughts and activities, rather than public events" (24). Bloom emphatically uses an omitted detail from Nin's personal life to argue that she, indeed, was intending to write for an audience. This particular critique, of the intricacies in the textual features and production of a diary, are often subject to biases, a moral judgment from critics of the diarist, rather than curiosity about the genre.

Crucially, Marlene Kadar writes in her essay, "Coming to Terms: Life Writing – from Genre to Critical Practice" (1992), that any autobiographical text, including the diary, is constructed by a range of discourses and literary conventions, as well as types of consciousness. Kadar evokes the image of the malleable qualities of water that in turn assumes the shape of its vessel (11). To suggest that the diary as a genre holds the possibility of illusion, of the slant qualities of reality, is a reminder that the reader must prepare for the possibilities and pleasures of being tricked. The diary as a literary genre holds the fertile possibilities of the trickstar/trickster archetype, discussed in detail in Chapter 3, when I turn to the myth of the diarist.

Conclusion: how we read matters

Clearly, to many scholars, autobiography values unification of self, a sense of authority on one's life and narrative while pursuing a heroic quest. As for diaries, another form of self-life writing, a polyvocal sense of self carries the narrative through gaps, and, as inherent to the genre, tensions between myth, fantasy, metaphor and self arise. Reading diaries requires us to consider complexities and crossroads where "a thousand characters" emerge, and social and cultural constructs intersect within the text. We should also remember that when reading diaries, one is engaged in reading a text that, despite its roots in the private, is nonetheless concerned with craft and aesthetics. In this event, we are called to rethink literary standards and better understand that how we read diaries matters. In her diaries, Nin's exploration of the conflicting roles within a patriarchal order, and the desire for a creative selfhood, informs the complex construction of a new mythology by which to live. My interdisciplinary study provides an understanding of the narrative link between myth, metaphor and Nin's self-plotting in a literary sense. It is my hope that this investigation will provide new insights into the relationship between gender, genre, and mythopoesis in her writing.

Notes

1 In *Jung: A Feminist Revision*, specifically Chapter 2, "Introducing Jungian Theory," Susan Rowland analyzes Jung's definition of personal myth within the context of his work. Rowland describes grand theories as her term for the propensity in Jung's writings to "produce comprehensive accounts of the human psyche and culture," p. 177.

2 See C. G. Jung's *The Red Book: Liber Novus*. Ed. Sonu Shamdasani. New York: W.W. Norton. 2009. Print.

3 A method of literary criticism that emphasizes the historicity of a text by relating it to the social configurations of power or ideology in a given time.

Works cited

Baring, Anne and Jules Cashford. *The Myth of the Goddess: Evolution of an Image*. New York: Penguin Books. 1991. Print.

Benstock, Shari. "The Female Self Engendered: Autobiographical Writing and Theories of Selfhood." *Women and Autobiography*. Eds. Martine Watson Brownley and Allison B. Kimmich. Wilmington: Scholarly Resources Inc. 1999. Print.

Bloom, Lynn Z. "I Write for Myself and Strangers": Private Diaries as Public Documents." *Inscribing the Daily: Critical Essays on Women's Diaries*. Eds. Suzanne L. Bunkers and Cynthia A. Huff. Amherst: U of Massachusetts P. 1996. Print.

Burney, Fanny. *The Early Diary of Frances Burney*, (1768–1778). Ed. Annie Raine Ellis. London: Dent. 1907. Print.

Fothergill, Robert A. *Private Chronicles: A Study of English Diaries*. London: Oxford UP. 1974. Print.

Gannett, Cinthia. *Gender and the Journal: Diaries and Academic Discourse*. Albany: State U of New York P. 1992. Print.

Gusdorf, Georges. "Conditions and Limits of Autobiography." *Autobiography: Essays Theoretical and Critical*. Ed. James Olney. Princeton: Princeton UP. 1980. Print.

Hillman, James. *Re-visioning Psychology*. New York: Harper & Row. 1975. Print.

———. "In: Hestia's Preposition." *Mythic Figures*. Putnam: Spring Publications. 2007. Print.

Hinz, Evelyn J. Ed. *A Woman Speaks: The Lectures, Seminars, and Interviews of Anaïs Nin*. Chicago: Swallow Press. 1975. Print.

———. "Mimesis: The Dramatic Lineage of Auto/Biography." *Essays on Life Writing: From Genre to Critical Practice*. Toronto: Toronto UP. 1992. Print.

Jackson, Anna. *Diary Poetics: Form and Style in Writers' Diaries, 1915–1962*. New York: Routledge. 2010. Print.

Jung, C. G. *Memories, Dreams, Reflections*. New York: Random House. 1989. Print.

Kadar, Marlene. "Coming to Terms: Life Writing – from Genre to Critical Practice." *Essays on Life Writing: From Genre to Critical Practice*. Toronto: Toronto UP. 1992. Print.

Nin, Anaïs. *The Diary of Anaïs Nin Volume Three (1939–1944)*. New York: Harvest. 1969a. Print.

———. *The Diary of Anais Nin Volume Two (1934–1939)*. New York: Harvest. 1969b. Print.

———. *The Diary of Anaïs Nin Volume Five (1947–1955)*. New York: Harvest. 1969c. Print.

———. *The Diary of Anaïs Nin Volume Seven (1966–1974)*. New York: Harvest. 1969d. Print.

Olney, James. "Autobiography and the Cultural Moment: A Thematic, Historical and Bibliographical Introduction." *Autobiography: Essays Theoretical and Critical*. Ed. James Olney. Princeton: Princeton UP, 1980. Print.

———. "A Theory of Autobiography." *Autobiography: Essays Theoretical and Critical*. Princeton: Princeton UP. 1980.

Podnieks, Elizabeth. *Daily Modernism: The Literary Diaries of Virginia Woolf, Antonia White, Elizabeth Smart, and Anaïs Nin*. London: McGill-Queen's UP. 2000. Print.

Simons, Judy. *Diaries and Journals of Literary Women from Fanny Burney to Virginia Woolf*. Iowa City: Iowa UP. 2001. Print.

Smith, Sidonie and Julia Watson, Ed. *Women, Autobiography, Theory: A Reader*. London: Wisconsin UP. 1998. Print.

Smith, Zadie. *Changing My Mind: Occasional Essays*. New York: Penguin Books. 2009. Print.

Stanton, Domna C. *The Female Autography*. New York: C.U.N.Y. 1984. Print.

Woolf, Virginia. *The Diary of Virginia Woolf, Volume 1 (1915–1919)*. Ed. Anne Olivier Bell. New York: Harvest. 1977. Print.

———. *The Diary of Virginia Woolf, Volume 3 (1925–1930)*. Ed. Anne Olivier Bell. New York: Harvest. 1980. Print.

Chapter 2

Anaïs Nin's expurgated diaries *Volume One* (1931–1934) and *Two* (1934–1939)

Modernism and mythopoesis

> Man created a world cut off from nature. Woman has to create within the mystery, storms, terrors, the infernos of sex, the battle against abstractions and art. She has to sever herself from the myth man creates, from being created by him, she has to struggle with her own cycles, storms, terrors which man does not understand.
>
> (Anais Nin 1937)

Virginia Woolf's (1882–1941) work often questioned the gender context of writing, and it serves as a reminder of the historical and material conditions of the early Modernist period in which Woolf lived. Woolf joined the critical discussion of the social history of women's lives. In her review of "The Women Novelists," by R. Brimley Johnson, she observed: "As Mr. Brimley Johnson again and again remarks, a woman's writing is always feminine; it cannot help being feminine; at its best it is most feminine: the only difficulty lies in defining what we mean by feminine" (26). It was a literary world maintained by societal structures that believed creativity to be the gift and birthright of a man. Eliot, writing in 1917, validates this sentiment: "I struggle to keep the writing as much as possible in Male hands, as I distrust the Feminine in Literature" (Lee 433). Women who took up writing careers often had to carve out the time between domestic duties to write. When permitted into literary circles, women had to be further concerned with alienating men, and being accused of either the masculinization or over-feminization of their own work. Consequently, for a woman, claiming the right to a life of letters came at a higher price than for a man. Anaïs Nin (1903–1977) expresses the tension of these sexism structures of society as emblematic of a disharmony between the womb, "life flow" and objective and abstraction in art and language governed by "imitations of phalluses." Nin saw the "withering" world, created and authored by patriarchy, as sustaining remnants of a wasteland (2:235). Consequently, both Woolf and Nin, and other Modernist women writers, were aware that to be an artist meant creating not only a new language, but a cultural landscape conducive for women to create.

Here I argue for the value of rethinking the history and scope of Modernism to include late Modernist writer Anaïs Nin. Uncovering the traditionally absent voices of female experiences in the intellectual context of modern history contributes to re-visioning Modernism. This excavation is essential, as Shari Benstock suggests in *Women of the Left Bank: Paris, 1900–1940*, "once women Modernists are placed beside their male colleagues, the hegemony of masculine heterosexual values that have for so long underwritten our definitions of Modernism is put into question" (Benstock 6). Broadening the literary backdrop of Modernism, to be inclusive of diverse voices such as Nin's, helps us to reflect on the literary movement through a vastly wider panoramic view different from the canon chiefly comprised of men.

From a feminist perspective, the early Modernist canon in particular encrypts a predominantly white, male perspective, and a few white women. Core Modernist writers of the early canon of 1910 through the mid-1940s have been held to be Marcel Proust, D. H. Lawrence, James Joyce, T. S. Eliot, Ezra Pound, Virginia Woolf, Dorothy Richardson and William Faulkner (Scott 6). This literary canon distorts the history of 20th-century Modernist literature. Not only is the scope of Modernism greater, but women were publishing in unique Modernist styles, including unique mythopoetic modes, well through the 1940s. The traditional description of Modernism characterizes it as involving the life and literature of Europe in the period roughly between the two World Wars, 1914–1945. In her critique of this traditional description, Sheri Benstock, in *Women's Writing in Exile*, argues for its misconstruction and oversight. That is, the traditional definition tends to imply that its evolution was situated in European cities, particularly Paris, London and Berlin. American Modernists, it is suggested, absconded their lives and headed to live and work abroad (Benstock 20). This detail excludes the fact that Modernism is an international movement, meaning countries all over the world explored their own forms of Modernism and had their thriving practices.[1]

Also, as Benstock notes, the canonized definition of Modernism would have us believe that the literary movement was shaped in reaction to cultural-social-political power structures that contributed to the war. Yet some Modernist aspects do uphold societal constructs and standards. This often includes the preservation practiced by Eliot, Pound and Wyndham Lewis, for example (Benstock 22). Also, traditional definitions of Modernism posit that it was a war-related literary movement. These traditional characteristics of literary Modernism overlook critical details, as they eliminate women in major ways: women were not necessarily on the frontlines of war, and women generally did not have access to a classical education which would have given them exposure to the same modern world as was provided for most men (Benstock 22). With this, Benstock argues that female Modernist writing warrants its own attention and definition, reminding us that Modernism includes a range of literary practices that unfolded "through various stages of Modernism" (22). While women were writing about war – for example, Edith Wharton wrote several books about the war: *Fighting France: From Dunkerque to Belfort* (1915), *The Marne* (1918), *French Ways and Their Meaning* (1919), and *A Son at the Front* (1923) – their accounts were dismissed as merely spectatorial.[2] When reviewed by men, these works were mocked, particularly *A Son at the Front*, as its depiction of war was considered "too 'removed' to be pertinent" (Benstock 27). The tendency was to view women as unauthorized to depict war experiences, especially compared to those captured by men. Thus, underscoring the war(s) as a prominent characteristic of Modernist literature is not only contentious, but also problematically limiting to the definition of Modernism. Yet a critical question is how did Modernist women writers represent their cultural, social, literary, and political viewpoints, including those related to war? A close look at Nin's literary credo, which I develop in Chapter 4, reveals that her political attitude was focused on individual responsibility to self as a way to contribute to the collective. For example, when asked about her outlook on the effects of collective conflict, Nin's response was:

> I think if we come back to the concept of a small and intimate universe and then realized that what we call the communal life or mass movements are really aggregates of individuals and that the more developed, the more expanded, the deeper, the more poetic, the more free the individual is, then the mass, the larger movements, would take on a different character.
>
> (Hinz 13)

The backdrop of war compelled Nin to resort to psychological theories, and at times religious imagery, as a method to transgress the tension between her relationship with politics, patriarchal structures that oppress women, and her own creativity.

For some of the other women Modernists, such as Natalie Barney, Sylvia Beach, Nancy Cunard, Janet Flanner, Adrienne Monnier and Virginia Woolf, World War I "solidified a commitment to liberal causes and fear of repressive and inhumane political power structures" (Benstock 31). The context of war created an "emergent consciousness of marginalism," which would result in "psychological collapse (in the case of Woolf and Cunard) and to reversal of values as evidenced in anti-Semitism and political reactionism (Gertrude Stein and Natalie Barney)" (Benstock 31). What the amalgam of reactions to the war and other themes, capturing the wasteland of Modernism, tells us is that Modernism as a literary movement did not produce a single depiction of the social and political, or any, elements of the historical context of the time.

With an emphasis on Nin's literary opus, the critical questions that ground this study are: what does Nin's work tell us about Modernist women's experiences, as captured through her literary representations, and what do these representations reveal about the cultural context in which they were constructed? While the scope of my focus is on Nin's work, it is not my contention that Nin's works are emblematic of what all Modernist women were preoccupied with, nor do I make the assumption that gender alone points to the differences in literary methods during Modernism. Rather, I concur with Benstock when she maintains:

> Modernism constituted an overtly acknowledged literary movement . . . one whose aesthetic principles and literary claims were codified in a series of

> manifestos, whose texts were printed in journals specifically dedicated to the propagation of Modernist literature, and practice of Modernism was highly individualist, often anarchic, incorporating contradictory impulses under a single 'ism.'
>
> (32)

Late Modernism constitutes writers publishing in the years 1930–1945, including Anaïs Nin, who was born in Paris on February 21, 1903, and then returned to her native city in the early 1930s, but was uprooted in 1939 at the start of World War II. While in Paris, Nin become part of the thriving artistic community, specifically on the Left Bank, in the early 20th century (Benstock 4). Other Modernist women writers in Paris between 1900–1940 include Margaret Anderson, Djuna Barnes, Natalie Barney, Sylvia Beach, Kay Boyle, Bryther (Winifred Ellerman), Colette, Caresse Crosby, Nancy Cunard, Hilda Doolittle (H.D.), Janet Flanner, Jane Heap, Maria Jolas, Mina Loy, Adrienne Monnier, Jean Rhys, Solita Solano, Gertrude Stein, Alice B. Toklas, Renee Vivien and Edith Wharton.[3]

Modernism did not produce one unique brand of mythopoesis. In fact, during the early Modernist period, there was concern with how one rendered selfhood in literature, and the ponderable link between life and art produced an artistic tension of whose perspective, and personal myth, was allowed to penetrate the white, male, heterosexual literary world. Two prominent impulses preoccupying Nin's own literary creed are, indeed, the connection between the personal and the collective through mythic tropes in art. Two seminal works suggestively capture this topic that ensued in early Modernism: "*Ulysses*, Order and Myth" (1923) by T. S. Eliot, and "Modern Fiction" (1925) by Virginia Woolf. While scholars offer in-depth analyses of the early Modernist canon of 1910 to the 1930s, my purpose here is to focus on these two essays as pillars of Anglo-American Modernism, which subsequently informed the artistic climate of Nin's milieu.

In his essay "*Ulysses*, Order and Myth," published in 1923, T. S. Eliot compliments James Joyce's *Ulysses* as one of the most important books of the age to which Modernism is anchored (175). For Eliot, a central question for the Modernist writer is the extent to which "one can be classical in tendency by doing the best one can with the material at hand," that is, the writer's own spontaneous flow of life. Eliot extols Joyce's ability to impose a mythic form on a contemporary experience through an impersonal tradition rather than his own subjective structure. The brilliance in Joyce's work, according to Eliot, is its use of "the mythic mode: a continuous parallel between contemporaneity and antiquity" (177). This mythic mode is a way of "controlling" and "organizing" content that links contemporary history to an inherited form (177). In this case, Eliot sees that "in using the myth, in manipulating a continuous parallel between contemporaneity and antiquity, Mr. Joyce is pursuing a method which others must pursue after him" (177). Doing so, according to Eliot, reveals an astute ability to control order to provide a significant perspective into modernity. In advocating an impersonal and less introspective

"I," and by referencing a specific lineage of antiquity, Eliot overlooks severe limitations of his proposed mythic method.

Briefly, Eliot's emphasis on the role of myth in "control" and "order" is a concern for Laurence Coupe in his book *Myth.* Coupe reads Eliot's use of "myth" in his review of *Ulysses* as synonymous with the word "tradition," to strictly mean applying an ancient paradigm upon disorder. Eliot, Coupe notes, believes that Joyce was able to understand the chaos of modernity by imposing an ancient paradigm on literature. That is, Eliot "invoked the spatial, impersonal tradition rather than expressed his temporal, personal interests" (36). Also, Coupe rightly reminds the reader that ancient Greeks separated knowledge into *mythos*, signifying story, and *logos*, meaning truth. *Mythos* came to imply fantasy and *logos* rational argument (9). By referring to Aristotle's *Poetics*, wherein he interprets *mythos* to mean "emplotment," emphasizing "imaginary story as well as plot," Coupe argues that Western modernity has come to privilege *logos* over *mythos* (39). In Eliot's response to *Ulysses* we see that he privileges form over tale, structure over story. By overlooking the *mythos* in the sense of "the narrative process of psychic exploration" (51), Eliot "wants only order, and tries to abstract the 'pure' myth informing Joyce's novel from the given sequence of events and interaction of characters" (39). Coupe notes that the *mythos* of Homer becomes the *logos*, the truth in the structure, which Joyce is recognized as imposing on his material.

Moreover, Eliot does not value just any order, as his telling examples reveal. The "mythic method" he is praising is "already adumbrated by Mr. Yeats" (311). Eliot approves of Modernist writers drawing from "tradition," including the aesthetics of myth, as providing modern art with a path to redemption. By referring to Yeats's own mythic ideas – in *A Vision* – as another classic example, Jerome J. McGann, in his essay "'The Grand Heretics of Modern Fiction' Laura Riding, John Cowper Powys, and the Subjective Correlative," points out that "Eliot's 'mythic method' is limited by its neo-classicist ethos" (311). Eliot suggests the recollection and connection to "ancient paradigm" belongs only to an exclusive elite. This selective attitude, and sexism, regarding what is deemed valuable in modern literature is also exemplified in Eliot's rash response to the work of Gertrude Stein (1874–1946).

In a review published in *The National and Athenequem* in 1927, titled "Charleston, Hey! Hey!" Eliot mocked Gertrude Stein's style and called it "intolerable" (McGann 311). Eliot felt Stein's work was "not improving, it is not assuming, it is not interesting, it is not good for one's mind. But its rhythms have a peculiar hypnotic power not met with before . . . But this is the future in which we ought not to be interested" (McGann 311). While Eliot acknowledges the rhythms of Stein's prose, he sees it as flawed and dissuades against pursuing it as a method to follow in the future. McGann points out that for Eliot, "The focus in Stein is not on some conceptual or thematic result of the writing but on the act of writing itself" (312). By suggesting that the value in modern literature should be what can be created through an objective lens, and by further promoting the rigid ordering of mythic ideas in its neo-classicist ethos, the mythic method Eliot praises excludes other, more fluid subject positions and literary styles.

Furthermore, this "mythic method" reveals a brutish limitation in its exclusivity and attempt to perpetuate the already white male perspectives of the times. Elizabeth Podnieks, in *Daily Modernism: The Literary Diaries of Virginia Woolf, Antonia White, Elizabeth Smart, and Anaïs Nin* (2000), reads Eliot's emphasis on "controlling" and "ordering" as the poet's own anxiety about the potential "feminization of literature" (79). Podnieks posits, as contended by Elaine Showalter in *Sexual Anarchy*, that by the 1880s, "women writers constituted a set of frightening rivals in the literary market place" (79). Consequently, what seemed to many like the feminization of literature resulted in identity problems for male artists as a part of the history of 20th-century literature (79). While Eliot valued mythology, religion and astrology as epistemological forms, the lineage of antiquity to which Eliot referred mostly excluded women of the time, since they had not enjoyed the same privileges of education. Many women would not have been introduced in the same way to past conventions, including literary traditions. Eliot was certainly not alone in this misogynist view. Ezra Pound denied the fact that women had made any meaningful contributions to literature at all. In the *New Age* journal, Ezra Pound (1885–1972) writes: "Not wildly anti-feminist, we are yet to be convinced that any woman ever invented anything in the arts" (Scott 79).[4] Women were thus excluded as important contributors of artistic models. Fortunately, Eliot's austere vision of imposing an ideal order is not the only characterization of myth and self in Modernism.

In contrast to Eliot's manifesto, Virginia Woolf offers an alternative perspective of the traditional methods of art in Modernist literature, including the relationship between self, myth and literature. Woolf strikes back at Eliot's narrow viewpoint, and she begins her essay "Modern Fiction," published in 1925, by criticizing the writer. She questions the extent to which life reveals itself in art, and reflects on the purpose and value of the need for the writer to control its design. She writes, "The writer seems constrained, not by his own free will but by some powerful and unscrupulous tyrant who has him in thrall, to provide a plot . . . The tyrant is obeyed; the novel is done to a turn" (160). Woolf cannot help but ask, "is life like this? Must novels be like this?" (160). Woolf's concern is a critique of Eliot's emphasis on the return to archaic structure as part of a mythic mode, and implicitly on his mythic aesthetics as an alternative to life and the writer's subjectivity. Woolf appears to appreciate the aesthetics derived from the writer's own life flow: "Let us record the atoms as they fall upon the mind in the order in which they fall, let us trace the pattern, however disconnected and incoherent in appearance, which each sight or incident scores upon the consciousness" (161). For Woolf, the writer needed to be guided by her own sequence of ideas and patterns of thought. In terms of the literary transformation of the quotidian, neither Woolf nor Nin saw such in opposition to psychic and poetic "patterns" from the writer's life from which to create art.

Woolf invites writers to look within without relinquishing the quotidian by "examin[ing] for a moment an ordinary mind on an ordinary day" (160). She explains, "The mind receives a myriad impressions – trivial, fantastic, evanescent, or engraved with the sharpness of steel" (160). Her emphasis on the "ordinary day" is reflected in works such as *Mrs. Dalloway*, another hallmark Modernist text, depicting the complexity of the protagonist's life as it unfolds in a single day. Nin, too, sets the plot of *Winter of Artifice* within a 24-hour day. Woolf's call for discarding conventions further emphasizes the individual and the irrational, rather than the controlled and logical. Also, Woolf's praise of Joyce's work reveals a different emphasis than that underscored in Eliot's review of Joyce. She admires the *mythos* in Joyce's work, and the way he explores psychic expression, "emplotment," as Aristotle and Coupe would say:

> Mr. Joyce is spiritual; he is concerned at all costs to reveal the flickering of that innermost flame which flashes its messages through the brain, and in order to preserve it he disregards with complete courage whatever seems to him adventitious, whether it be probability, or coherence, or any other of these signposts which for generations have served to support the imagination of a reader when called upon to imagine what he can neither touch nor see. (161)

Woolf brilliantly calls for modern fiction to include the personal, "that innermost flame," the psychological, the "trivial, fantastic, evanescent," that invites the mythopoetics of daily living, meaning the inner narratives, including the compulsive ones, that create meaning in our lives (164). Woolf values poetic composites derived from psyche and the emerging rhythm of the life of the artist. Noticeably, Nin recognized Woolf's approach as vital in literature: "It was Virginia Woolf who sought to restore to the novel not its familiar character structure, but the visionary insight of the poet" (*Novel of the Future* 59). While Woolf created more veiled autobiographical novels than Nin, both writers valued the orchestration between life and art through a mythopoesis of their own.

As seen in both Eliot's and Woolf's essays, while the early Modernist engaged and advocated the importance of self and myth in distinct methods, the struggle and argument for and against the inclusion of the personal and subjective world of the writer resulted in the devaluing of the feminine. These are the conditions in which Anaïs Nin, as a late Modernist writer, created her own brand of mythopoesis.

In her early works, Nin critiques Catholicism as a patriarchal institution that contributes to oppressive gender structures. She reflects on the tendencies of male writers, specifically Henry Miller and Lawrence Durrell, to uphold their own objectivity by assuming a God-like role as a creator: "All the nonsense Henry and Larry talked about, the necessity of 'I am God' in order to create (I suppose they mean 'I am God, I am not a woman'). Woman never had direct communication with God anyway, but only through man, the priest" (2:233). As a woman writing against dogmas, and between voices, Nin was aware of the extreme contingency of culture. She juxtaposes religious imagery and artistic creation against her experiences with gender constructs: "As to this 'I am God,' which makes creation as an act of solitude and pride, this image of God alone making sky, earth, sea, it is this image which has confused woman. Man too, because he thinks God did it all alone, and he thinks he did it all alone" (2:233–234). Nin sees the God concept of monotheisms, assuming control of his creation "as an act of solitude and pride," a God fantasy resulting in male hubris. For Nin, it was imperative to address this shortcoming as a means to create space for the soul of the female writer.

The preoccupation with objectivity in art, through depersonalization formed a tension that concerned and terrified many writers. Yet as a female writer, who sought out the subjectivity in dreams, psyche and her personal myth, it seems that Nin had more reason to be terrified. Nonetheless, Nin dared to find a mythic and symbolic mode already within the psyche. For Nin, "the power to re-create lies in the sensibilities rather than intellectual memory or observation" (*The Novel of the Future* 159). This historical context for Nin's writing provides insight that Modernism did not produce just a solitary brand of mythopoesis. Hence, we are further reminded that the mythic mode Eliot extolled was simply "*a* 'mythic mode'" not "*the* 'mythic mode,'" as justly noted by Coupe (43).

Emplacement of the literary diary in Modernist traditions elucidates meaning of the genre for the Modernist diarist. Elizabeth Podnieks, in *Daily Modernism: The Literary Diaries of Virginia Woolf, Antonia White, Elizabeth Smart, and Anaïs Nin*, offers her insight:

> Modernist writers, specifically diarists, may have confronted and then abandoned male myths of women, adopting their own versions of female experience. But at times they may have embraced these myths, which prescribed how they should perceive themselves as daughters, wives, mothers, and lovers. Whether Woolf, White, Smart, and Nin seem to be challenging or accepting, radical or conservative, they were perpetually struggling with their selves as they tried to make sense of and reconcile traditional gender roles with recent dismantlings of gender construction. These struggles were enacted on the diary site, which is at once a textual battlefield, a playground, and a no man's land.
>
> (65)

Modernist women writers navigated the complexities of a system of gender and used their art to characterize and make visible the unique difficulties they faced as women and artists. Their diaries were often used to pose questions of inspiration and authorship. This means that for Woolf and Nin, who also wrote in more canonical literary forms, their literary diaries offer insight into their credos. Also, the intimacy with self, as explored in the diary, helped both Woolf and Nin synchronize with their respective visions of the world, as both preferred introverted characters who delve into the tensions of self-reflection, including multiple sensibilities, in the quest for meaning. But unlike Nin, Woolf's views on psychoanalysis were unfortunately shaped by her harsh experiences with psychiatric institutions. Her art, therefore, tended to veil direct references to psychoanalysis more than Nin's.[5] Nevertheless, thoughts of both Nin's and Woolf's characters are depicted through stream of consciousness to convey their interior lives.

What is more, Nin was keenly aware of her own subject position as a female writer, and of the wasteland, both interior and exterior, prevalent in the landscape. For Nin, the patriarchal wasteland posed a dilemma tied to femininity. According to Nin the female writer "has to sever herself from the myth man creates, from being created by him, she has to struggle with her own cycles, storms, terrors which man does not understand" (2:234). It was by fusing her creative urge with a mythic consciousness that Nin investigates the feminine.

It was Nin's contention that art needed to "battle against abstractions" in order to embody a creativity that reflected the raw material of the writer, including the mysteries of life. For Nin, this meant tethering her art to life. Alchemizing and birthing a new myth was a way to create art that surpassed the abstractions privileged in a sky-father world. An analysis of Nin's mythic tropes that engage a personal sense of self is the subject of the rest of this and subsequent chapters in this book. However, now it is necessary to consider a more immediate framework for Nin's work: the then-emerging field of psychoanalysis and surrealism.

Psychology, surrealism, personal myth and the literary diary

The rising interest in psychology in the early 20th century has been credited with providing an opportunity to dialogue with artists exploring the "I" in autobiographical writings, including diaries (Podnieks 89). By the 20th century, men were increasingly associated with public space and the creation of culture, and not psychological introspection (Podnieks 88). Also, in the first decades of the 20th century, Freud's subject of research included hysteria, dreams and the workings of the unconscious. Freud's early following tended to first be women, as men were "perhaps less interested in psychology because of this feminization of it, and because Freud himself was preoccupied with the female gender" (Podnieks 89). Freud's psychological views contributed to the dichotomization of gender that was consistent with traditional views: men were prescribed to the sphere of the public, and women stereotypically associated with inner life, the domain of the home. Given the circumstances of this exacerbated gender divide at the time, it is not surprising that the diary would serve, and be more socially accepted, as a genre for women than for men (Podnieks 46). In this manner, women have come to understand how genre and subversion operate to provide a true image of themselves.

Nin's early exposure to psychoanalysis was around 1928, introduced through her cousin Eduardo Sánchez. In her early diary (1927–1931) she remarks: "The science was utterly unknown to me until the day I met Eduardo in New York. He told me almost immediately that he was being psychoanalyzed and that at last he knew what was wrong with him" (*Linotte* 4). It is onboard the *S.S. Mauretania* from New York back to Paris that Nin makes a pivotal link between the world the diary was swinging wide open for her and that of psychology. She reflects: "I have just discovered a new justification of my Journal . . . I owe to it what some people owe to psychology: knowledge of myself, extreme consciousness of what in others is vague, of my weaknesses, of my dreams, of my talents" (*Linotte* 4). She always seemed aware that the impetus of her craft as a writer was propelled by a desire to find expression of the subjective, and in some ways the inner world. Nin becomes increasingly interested in the developing field of psychology in the ensuing years between 1928 and 1934.

Her direct involvement with psychoanalysis began around 1932, first with Dr. René Allendy, who at the time was her cousin Eduardo's analyst (Harms 112). Allendy was a protégé of Freud who helped develop the Paris Psychoanalytic Society in 1926 (Harms 112). One year later, in 1933, the time of Nin's troubling reconnection with her long-absent father Joaquin Nin, she read Otto Rank's book *Art and Artist: Creative Urge and Personality Development,* and began her patient/therapist relationship with Rank. He was Nin's analyst for 10 months, from November 1933 to around August 1934. Indeed, in the fall of 1934 Nin practiced lay psychoanalysis in New York, under Rank's supervision. In April 1935, Nin made the difficult decision of leaving New York to return to Paris. Nin reflected on this decision: "Rank was asking for another sacrifice: to give up my writing and rewrite his books. He saw me thin and worn and yet he disapproved of my leaving New York" (2:38).[6] Nin ends *Volume One* of her diaries by explaining the crucial role psychology had during the early years of her life: "Psychoanalysis did save me because it allowed the birth of the real me, a most dangerous and painful one for a woman, filled with dangers; for no one has ever loved an adventurous woman as they have loved adventurous men" (1:359–360). A deep and complex relationship between the two lasted until Rank's death in 1939 (Spencer 97). The significance of this relationship, along with other important events in Nin's cultural context in 1932–1934 are expounded on in Chapter 4.

Nin's exploration of interior landscapes, energized by dreams and psyche, invoked C. G. Jung's notion of personal myth captured in two aphorisms: first, "proceed from the dream outward," and later, "the personal life, deeply lived, takes you beyond the personal" (*The Novel of the Future* 159). It was Nin's contention that following human "patterns" that make up a dynamic life was a way to reach the archetypal. In Nin's world, there were two central human necessities that linked life and art: the first was the desire to be "intimate with experiences," as witnessed in her diary. The second need involved the archetypal created through "the myth of our lives," depicted in her fiction, as I discuss in Chapters 4 and 5 (*A Woman Speaks* 190). Later in her life, Nin offered some clarification as to the prominent psychological theorist who influenced her: "It wasn't Jung I was interested in so much as Otto Rank's interest in the creative will and the artist" (*A Woman Speaks* 136). Nin's interest in dreams and mythic narratives that shape our lives, along with the rejection of formulas, and of mere rational approaches and conventional modes of creating art, harmonized with the emerging psychological approaches to psyche, sexuality and creativity of the time.

Another important context that intertwined with Nin's work is her fascination and encounters with Surrealism. Although Nin was never an official member of the Surrealist movement, she was attracted to the Surrealist emphasis on searching for "the marvelous, a way of filling life and creation with surprise, a way of heightening life and infusing it with meaning" (*The Novel of the Future* 16). In an interview in the summer of 1973, Nin reflects on the fact that "Surrealism was part of the air [they] breathed" (Hinz 207). She was drawn to André Breton, the father of Surrealism, author of *The Surrealist Manifesto* (1924), and the emphasis that art should include automatic and spontaneous experiences, including dreams as a rich reservoir for artistic creation. As quoted in Bettina L. Knapp's book *Anaïs Nin*, Surrealism, according to the manifesto, was defined as, "a liberating and constructive force, one that would free man from the grasping tentacles of an overly constricting, moralist bourgeois society as well as from literary and artistic conventions" (Knapp 40). Specifically, Nin was interested in how surrealism reached far beyond formulas, as detailed in author Antonin Artaud's work. In March of 1933 Allendy introduces Nin to Artaud, whom she would come to refer to as a literary "twin." In a diary entry, Nin describes Artaud as, "The man-dreamer, diabolical and innocent, frail, nervous, potent. As soon as our eyes meet I am plunged into my imaginary world. He is veritably haunted and haunting. I was afraid to meet him, because a few days before I had read some of his writing and there was an extraordinary twinship" (*Incest*: 118–119). In another encounter with Artaud that same month, Nin shares with him a copy of *House of Incest*. She refers to it as the book "though written before I knew you, was written to synchronize with your vision of the world" (1:188). For the next year or so, Nin immerses herself in Artaud's works such as "Theatre and the Plague," which was informed by the Theatre of Cruelty.[7] Surrealism provided an important literary context for Nin to pursue her own creative process, including her interests in capturing and defining the "marvelous" in her literary world (1:5). Ultimately, for Nin, the Surrealists' "way of approaching a multilevel, multifaceted, multidimensional state" was a source of inspiration in the early 1930s (*The Novel of the Future* 38).

Nin pursued, along with the creative means in her milieu, a desire to create and revolutionize directly from her subject position as a woman, as she was clearly aware of the need for the recognition of women's contributions to fill a cultural void. In a diary entry, Nin paraphrases Otto Rank: "We know very little about women. In the first place, it was men who invented 'the soul.' Man was the philosopher and the psychologist, the historian and the biographer. Woman could only accept man's classifications and interpretations. The woman who played important roles thought like men, and wrote like men" (1:276). Nin understood that women's literary achievements have been absent from historical sources. Thus, her literary achievements would contribute a pivotal voice and vision to recognize the role of women that has been distorted by historiography. To explore and imagine this vision, it would be necessary for Nin, along the way, to descend into the depths of psyche.

Bettina L. Knapp notes that Nin's interest in Surrealism stems from her deep desire to use art to alchemize her own wounds resulting from her father's sexual abuse of her, as well as his abandonment of the entire family. "She wanted to gain self-knowledge and used art and language as the means to restore psychic balance in her life," writes Knapp (43). Similarly, Elizabeth Podnieks, in *Daily Modernism: The Literary Diaries of Virginia Woolf, Antonia White, Elizabeth Smart, and Anaïs Nin*, points out that it was the surrealist work by Artaud that helped Nin dramatize her psyche during a particularly challenging and dark time of her life in the years 1932 to 1933 (322). I expound on this important reference in Chapter 4.

It is clear that Surrealism offered Nin a portal through which to pursue not only her own interests in the wavering nature of truth and self, but a way to explore the *prima materia*, prime matter, used for the alchemical process of turning all other matter into gold, which symbolically includes psychic wounds she long contended with as a woman and as a writer. Psychology was a prosperous map to help Nin better understand the cacophonies of interior and exterior experiences that were central to her interest in literature. Importantly, together Surrealism and psychology provided the context for her to create a textual account of incest from a woman's perspective. I will develop this point in Chapter 4. For now, it is important to recall that Nin's mythopoetic style is emboldened with embodied experiences, metaphors, dreams, myths and fantasies, that "flow" both in and out of Nin's life, as well as through the souls of her characters.

A womb of her own: creation myth within personal myth

One of my arguments in this book is that Nin's use of the diary as a "playground of subjectivities" was fundamentally determined by an emerging and fluctuating confidence in herself as a female artist (Podnieks 66). Nin believed her exploration of personal myth, as derived from the creative depths of a feminine subject position, to be previously uncharted within traditional female literary expressions. Nin fought against androcentric ideologies. The "life flow" that she sought to capture in her diary, as well as in her fiction, resonates with what Virginia Woolf advocated in her early Modernist manifesto, "Modern Fiction." Like Woolf, Nin was concerned with charting a literary space that was inclusive, yet unique from the male-constructed myths for women at the time. Their characters explore experiences through interior monologues in sequential thoughts to convey mysterious tones and complex plots. In this way, Nin too was pioneering a new voice inclusive of embodiment, and of "the cellular miracle," within the writer's psyche (Zinnes 59).

In her notable essay "Art, the Dream, the Self," Harriet Zinnes, points out that Nin's early "criticism of Henry Miller's *Tropic of Capricorn*, for example, stems from her antagonism to an art that has abstracted that relation of womb to phallus" (Zinnes 57). Nin ponders, "Henry working on *Capricorn* writing about sex, blind to all but sex, writing like a maniac about sex" (2:256). And later writes: "I glance over what Henry was writing in *Tropic of Capricorn*, and there it was, the great anonymous, depersonalized world of sex. Instead of investing each woman with a different face, he takes pleasure in reducing all women to a biological aperture" (2:260). Nin's vision of art sought clarity of self through the personal as opposed to the "depersonalized" world she witnessed Henry Miller creating. She also reflects: "There are moments in Henry's talk when I feel truly tired, like a woman reaching for knowledge beyond her capacity. I stretch my mind to follow the curves and sweeps of man's mind. It is always the big, impersonal spaces which frighten me, the vast deserts, universe, cosmologies" (1:158). Nin describes attaining "knowledge" in a patriarchal world as a pursuit amidst the "impersonal spaces" through "curves" and "sweeps." It seems that in contrast, Nin's quest for knowledge and creativity is a somatic experience involving descending, "terror," "storms," as she searches for her own methods. Her diaries record the isolation she felt as she pursued and declared her own "cosmologies," along with the resistance she was up against in her male-centric literary circle in the early 1930s:

> I am puzzling over the meaning of things which do not perplex Gonzalo, I am gnawed by feelings unknown to Henry, troubled by questions neither Rank nor Allendy could answer, writing only in a diary which Henry says should be nailed with a big nail on the wall of his studio and muted forever, and I ask myself is it fear on the part of man, fear of a woman unveiling her own truths? Is there another reason for everyone being against it, one not purely ideological?
>
> (2:253)

Nin's diary was met with disapproval by those whose opinions she valued. In a diary entry Nin writes: "The diary goes on, but I need faith. This continuous attack on it, as a disease by Rank, as anti-art by Henry, wears me down" (2:235). The distorted feedback she received resulted in tension that persisted when creating her own artistic creed alongside male ideologies.

Nonetheless, Nin's persistence in writing her diary, which lasted over 60 years, tells us that she was propelled by an insistent desire to both develop her voice as a writer and speak truths previously unspoken. Nin was keenly aware, as noted by Zinnes, that "self-revelation is the first step towards revelation of the other" (58). It is by creating a "livable" world, one of resolute personal values that linked Nin to greater humanity. This was Nin's response to the wasteland of her social context.

I now return to a point I made in Chapter 1 formulated by C. G. Jung in *Memories, Dreams, Reflections* to deepen an understanding of the role of personal myth in the construction of a sense of "self" for Nin the diarist. I have stated that Nin's subjective engagement in her diaries with self, language and personal myth, specifically the *prima materia* in her diaries, can be contextualized within C. G. Jung's notion that the inner experiences pave the way towards becoming conscious of one's psychic process furthering self-realization. C. G. Jung used the term "personal myth" to point out that his own personal history of the self-realization of his unconscious was told as a myth. According to Jung, "myth is more individual and expresses life more precisely than does science" (3). Ultimately, for Jung, the "myth" in personal myth was a way to link the personal and the cultural. Jung posited that "what we are to our inward vision, and what man appears to be *sub specie aeternitatis*, can only be expressed by way of myth" (3). For Nin, the way to experience an "inward vision," as noted by Jung, was to "install" herself "inside the seed" as a way of coming into being (2:235). Nin's revealing description of becoming conscious of one's psychic process, through personal myth, is reminiscent of a vital motif in creation myth. For central to creation myth is the significance of coming into an embodied experience of relationship with oneself, as well as a greater community. Nin's use of this motif is a noteworthy intimation to her perception of personal myth, as it inter-relates with birth and the creative act.

To trace Nin's personal myth within her diaries, one must recall that her diaries are not constructed based on any one conventional literary model, and contain gaps in not only memory and time, but also between style and discourse. That is, the diarist reveals the creative unfolding of a presumable sense of self in the making, in which myth penetrates the writing space. It was essential for Nin to write in a literary form that linked female understanding with an internalized experience of the body. Consequently, the metaphor of the womb and its labyrinthine qualities is central for Nin's new myth for the female writer. As such, she creates from a descent "into the real womb" to "expose its secrets and its labyrinths" (2:235). It was her belief that the female writer both births and reclaims her voice stemming from a womb space where deeper truths of her being are born: "She must describe the voracious moods, the desires, the worlds contained in each cell of it. For the womb has dreams," writes Nin (2:235). Nin's mythic motifs are worth noting. The image of the womb as the birth place that holds the "secrets" and "labyrinths" is Nin's feminine approach to an embodied language; she uses her diary, as a literary form, that holds the fluidity of the womb, not anchored to preconceived structures. Nin responds to the disembodied, "withered" wasteland of her time by emphasizing embodiment, feminine subjectivity and voice. Nin flows between the gaps of memory that are created when constructing her sense of self as the "writing subject" (Benstock 8). What is more, it should be noted, Nin's feminine images of birthing a voice, and sense of self, do not belong to women in an essentialist way, but rather to the mythic trope of earth-mother consciousness, as explained by Ann Baring and Jules Cashford in their comprehensive investigation of the mother goddess in *The Myth of the Goddess: Evolution of an Image*. To this work I turn to next.

The diary as earth-mother consciousness

To further understand the role of embodied language and mythic motifs in relation to the diaries, it is useful to consider Ann Baring and Jules Cashford's work in *The Myth of the Goddess: Evolution of an Image.* Here they trace the evidence of two basic myths that are essential to our human experiences – first, the myth of the Goddess, and second, the myth of the hunter. It is proposed that each myth contains within it specific human instincts. For example, the myth of the goddess contains the instinct for relationships and meaning, while the myth of the hunter contains the instinct to survive. Also held within the myth of the hunter lies sky-father consciousness (39). Sky-father consciousness is gendered, represented as a god, and is based on separation from nature. Sky-father consciousness is no longer based on connecting (Eros), but on separating (Logos). The research of Baring and Cashford reveals that the earliest type of religious myth was of an earth goddess, but she was "gradually relegated to the unconscious psyche of humanity" (40). "Yet we can find the lost primordial myth scattered throughout the symbolic images, myths and fairy tales of every civilization, frequently unrecognized, often unconnected with each other, but always present" (40). It should be noted that in the original myth of the earth goddess, "she" precedes gender division, and the earth goddess is not a matriarch in the sense of an all-controlling female. Moreover, C. G. Jung's notion of the collective unconscious proposes that the collective history of human experience is in some form in the psyche as part of being human (41). Jung uses the metaphor of the collective unconscious, which is the common inheritance of archetypes that are shared by all human beings. Yet the archetypes manifest as such according to images anchored in a particular cultural and historical specificity.

One place to locate earth-mother consciousness is through images that reside in the human psyche. For example,

> wherever we find the cave, the moon, the stone, the serpent . . . the spiral, meander and labyrinth; the wild animals . . . rituals concerned with the fertility of the earth and of animals and human beings, and the journey of the soul to another dimension, then we are in the presence of the images that once enacted the original myth.
>
> (Baring 40)

The images that evoke earth-mother consciousness, as found in myths, personal myths, literature and fairy tales of every civilization, put us into contact with the original myth. When in contact with these images, we should once again be reminded that since earth-mother consciousness precedes the division of gender, we are not merely in the realm of an embodied matriarch, but rather within the "roots of consciousness in the 'womb of the mother' – the human soul" (41). By allowing such mythic motifs – the ancient symbolism of the womb of earth-mother consciousness, and the sacred symbol of the labyrinth – to guide us through an exploration of Nin's diaries, we can discern how the diary allowed and invited Nin to create a mythopoesis from her personal myth amidst patriarchal structures, privileging sky-father consciousness.

For Nin, the passageways that bore creativity for the female writer stemmed from the womb, birthing what is unconscious into the realm of the conscious. The Seneca creation myth, "How the World Began," Sky Woman is responsible for carrying seeds from the upper world to the lower world where she will create new life. She is entrusted with the germination of these seeds from which her entire people shall be born and nourished. In this newly created lower world, Sky Woman finds herself moving from the depths of dark deep soil, amidst flourishing life. She grows from the darkness into the light of consciousness, as stated in the creation myth: "At the root of the tree which she had grasped she sunk into the soil where she had fallen and this too began to grow until it formed a tree with all manner of fruits and flowers and bore a luminous orb at its top by which the new world became illuminated" (Parker 62). From the dark depths of the womb of the earth, and from within the soil in the underworld, Sky Woman, first living thing on earth, emerges into the world as First Woman.

A central theme in this creation myth is the process of nature's truest cycle of death and rebirth through embodiment associated with the world. The seeds Sky Woman transmits from one world to another contain not only vital nourishment in the form of food for the next generation, but are also a rich source of family stock, of ancestry. When Sky Woman sinks into the mysterious navel of the earth and "the soil," as we are told in the myth, "where she had fallen and this too began to grow," resembles Nin's metaphorical description of the way in which she herself awakens consciousness and comes into being. She "installs [her]self inside the seed" to construct her personal myth from a place flowing with life (2:235). By giving tangible form to the vitality of the seed, and by birthing a new order, the diary discloses not only the portrayal of the making of one woman, but a mythic possibility for a community, as seen in the Seneca creation myth.

In his essay "On the Relation of Analytical Psychology to Poetry," Jung had similar Modernist ideas about the role of the artist, nature and the powerful force that propels creation. He states, "The unborn work in the psyche of the artist is a force of nature that achieves its end either with tyrannical might or with the subtle cunning of nature herself, quite regardless of the personal fate of the man who is its vehicle" (75). Jung's reference to the inventive force that impels a creation through a body – a force also seen in the Seneca creation myth – is linked to a creative process in the diary. The theme of bodily consciousness and understanding of one's divinity resonates with the diarist, for the diary contains a record of the seeds of awakening toward somatic consciousness that connects mystery, the body, creativity and cosmic forces. It is in her diaries that Anaïs Nin arranges the cosmos in a language that constitutes her personal myth, and thus, creation myth is wholly alive within her mythopoesis. Nin considers the important link between creative awakening, myth, mystery and intuition when she writes: "My art must be like a miracle. Before it goes through the conduits of the brain and becomes an abstraction, a fiction, a lie. It must be for woman, more like a personified ancient ritual, where every spiritual thought was made visible, enacted, represented" (2:235). Nin's reference to the "personified ancient ritual" evokes, as seen in the Seneca creation myth, an indigenous way of knowing that involves a perpetual act of balance of one's discerning faculties with an intent of understanding self within the world. Nin evokes the Goddess that is earth-mother consciousness, a form of being that values intimacy with self and other, and where language is revered and linked to embodied experiences.

Helen Tookey, in her book *Anaïs Nin, Fictionality and Femininity: Playing a Thousand Roles*, makes a similar point by arguing that "The 'real womb,' as [Nin] puts it is simultaneously physical, mythic and metaphorical, able to serve as the imagistic focus of Nin's conceptions of her own creativity and femaleness" (160). I argue that Nin aligns herself with the creative act central to the labyrinths of the womb, as the life-transmitting nature of earth-mother consciousness. Nin attains her creative "knowledge" by pursuing the labyrinth of her own body, psyche and mind where creativity is "enacted" and "represented." It is, indeed, fitting that the diary as a place to construct one's cosmology would invite the recognition of an ancient form of consciousness, that of the earth mother.

Conclusion: seeds of consciousness

It is my argument in this chapter that through an exploration of feminine embodiment, personal myth and the symbolic residing in psyche, Nin created a mythic method of her own, contributing to Modernist literary traditions. It was her contention that literary creation emerged from a seed connected to the body, allowing a unity with sacred mysteries to emerge. The seed contains dual forces and darkness: consciousness and unconsciousness, light and darkness, the power of life and death. Contact with a seed of creation means regeneration and the possibility to be reborn, particularly in stages of understanding, as seen throughout the unfolding seven volumes of Nin's diaries. By asserting her own feminine-embodied world, Nin speaks to what "otherness" felt like in a world that devalued the feminine (Benstock 8). Framing Nin's work within the paradigm of earth-mother consciousness accentuates the polyphony of voices in her fiction and diaries. Also, this allows us to better understand that Nin created a personal myth, which provided an alternative to an over-valuing of the prominent sky-father way of knowing, represented with "phalluses" and privileging truths and binaries, so prevalent in her time. Now, it is necessary to descend into the navel of earth-mother consciousness through a close look at the trickstar/trickster as a key mythic trope in the diaries of Anaïs Nin.

Notes

1 See Amy Oliver. *Modernism in Latin America*. New York: Routledge. 2016.

2 As quoted in Benstock, *Women in the West Bank*, Paris, 1900-1940, p. 27. The subsequent quote is also on page 27.

3 See Sheri Benstock's study in *Women of the Left Bank: Paris, 1900–1940,* wherein she expounds on the rich social and literary context of these women's lives, as well as their literary contributions to Modernism as a literary movement.
4 In *Daily Modernism: The Literary Diary of Virginia Woolf, Antonia White, Elizabeth Smart, and Anaïs Nin*, Podnieks expounds on the implications of misogynist traditions in Modernist literature.
5 Suzanne Nalbantian's chapter "Distancing and Displacement in Virginia Woolf," in her book *Aesthetic Autobiography: From Life to Art in Marcel Proust, James Joyce, Virginia Woolf and Anaïs Nin* analyzes Woolf's relationship with life, self and autobiographical literature.
6 In her essay "Beyond Therapy: The Enduring Love of Anaïs Nin for Otto Rank" Sharon Spencer points out complexities in Nin's relationship with Rank and how such details have been written about. She offers an endnote referencing Dr. E. James Lieberman's autobiography on Rank.
7 See Elizabeth Podnieks's analysis of Nin's relationship with Artaud in *Daily Modernism: The Literary Diaries of Virginia Woolf, Antonia White, Elizabeth Smart, and Anaïs Nin.*

Works cited

Baring, Anne and Jules Cashford. *The Myth of the Goddess: Evolution of an Image*. New York: Penguin Books. 1991. Print.

Benstock, Shari. *Women of the Left Bank: Paris, 1900–1940*. Texas: Texas UP. 1986. Print.

———. *Women's Writing in Exile*. Chapel Hill: The U of North Carolina P. 1989. Print.

Coupe, Laurence. *Myth*. London: Routledge. 1997. Print.

Eliot, T. S. "*Ulysses*, Order and Myth." *Selected Prose of T.S. Eliot*. New York: Harcourt Brace Jovanovich. 1956. Print.

Harms, Valerie. "Anaïs and Her Analyst, Rank and Allendy: The Creative and Destructive Aspects." *Literary Perspectives*. Ed. Suzanne Nalbantian. New York: St. Martin's Press. 1997. Print.

Hinz, Evelyn J. Ed. *A Woman Speaks: The Lectures, Seminars, and Interviews of Anaïs Nin*. Chicago: Swallow Press. 1975. Print.

Jung, C. G. "On the Relation of Analytical Psychology to Poetry." *Modern Man in Search of a Soul*. New York: Harvest. 1933. Print.

———. *Memories, Dreams, Reflections*. New York: Random House. 1989. Print.

Knapp, Bettina L. *Anaïs Nin*. New York: Frederick Ungar Publishing. 1978. Print.

———. *Recollections of Anaïs Nin by Her Contemporaries*. Ed. Benjamin Franklin V. Athens: Ohio UP. 1996. Print.

Lee, Hermione. *Virginia Woolf*. New York: Alfred A. Knopf. 1997. Print.

McGann, Jerome J. " 'The Grand Heretics of Modern Fiction': Laura Riding, John Cowper Powys, and the Subjective Correlative." *Modernism/Modernity* 13.2 (2006): 309–323. Project MUSE. Web. 13 August 2014.

Nin, Anaïs. *The Novel of the Future*. New York: Collier Books. 1968. Print.

———. *The Diary of Anaïs Nin Volume One (1931–1934)*. New York: Harvest. 1969a. Print.

———. *The Diary of Anaïs Nin Volume Two (1934–1939)*. New York: Harvest. 1969b. Print.

———. *Linotte: The Early Diary of Anaïs Nin (1914–1920)*. New York: Harcourt Brace Jovanovich. 1978. Print.

———. *Incest: From A Journal of Love (1932–1934)*. New York: Harcourt Brace Jovanovich. 1992. Print.

Parker, Arthur C. *Seneca Myths and Folk Tales*. Lincoln: Nebraska UP. 1923. Print.

Podnieks, Elizabeth. *Daily Modernism: The Literary Diaries of Virginia Woolf, Antonia White, Elizabeth Smart, and Anaïs Nin*. London: McGill-Queen's UP. 2000. Print.

Scott, Bonnie Kime. *The Gender of Modernism*. Bloomington: Indiana UP. 1990. Print.

———. *Refiguring Modernism*. Vol. 1. Bloomington: Indiana UP. 1995. Print.

Spencer, Sharon. "Beyond Therapy: The Enduring Love of Anaïs Nin for Otto Rank." *Anaïs Nin: Literary Perspectives*. Ed. Suzanne Nalbantian. New York: St. Martin's Press. 1997. Print.

Tookey, Helen. *Anais Nin, Fictionality and Feminity: Playing a Thousand Roles*. Oxford: Oxford UP. 2003. Print.

Woolf, Virginia. *Mrs. Dalloway*. New York: Harcourt Brace Jovanovich. 1925. Print.

———. "Women Novelists." *Essays on Twentieth-Century Books and Authors by Virginia Woolf*. New York: Harvest. 1965. Print.

———. "Modern Fiction." *The Essays of Virginia Woolf. Vol. 4. 1925–1928*. London: The Hogarth Press. 1984. Print.

Zinnes, Harriet. "Art, the Dream, the Self." *Anaïs Nin: Literary Perspectives*. Ed. Suzanne Nalbantian. New York: St. Martin's Press. 1997. Print.

Chapter 3

Risks and tricks in the myth of the diarist

> Tell the truth but tell it slant
> Success in Circuit lies
> Too Bright for our infirm Delight
> The Truth's superb surprise
> As Lightning to the Children eased
> With explanation kind
> The Truth must dazzle Gradually
> Or every man be blind –
> (Emily Dickinson 1868)

In a diary entry for June 13, 1919, the 16-year-old Anaïs Nin reflects on the condensing of her sense of self into a written book, as she references her life as an "epilogue, an unfinished book" (Linotte 251). Later, in Volume One, Nin references the diary as a space to "relive" her "life in terms of a dream, a myth, an endless story" (1:89). This concept, the diary as a literary genre inextricably linked to performing the act of living, inclusive of dreams, myths and creativity, remained a profound theme in Nin's diaries. Underscoring that self is not revealed through mere consciousness, Nin knew that unlike the autobiographer, who initiates the act of self-life writing with the goal of a unified and knowable self, the diarist is Interested in relating self and narrative to the fluidity and plurality of experiences. This means that for Nin, the diary records a quest to know all facets of self.

Nin constantly re-examined the diary as a living presence, as a cultural artifact whose boundaries were perpetually broadened and reconstructed in order for her to explore her sense of multiplicity. Her exploration would extend the boundaries between self, psyche and genre. Nin captured this outlook when writing: "I have always been tormented by the image of multiplicity of selves. Some days I call it richness, and other days I see it as a disease, a proliferation as dangerous as cancer" (1:47). Nin's admissions of feeling "tormented" by the "multiplicity of self" related her interest to a psychological exploration of integrating both artist and woman, along with the other constructs and categories assigned to her gender, such as wife, mother, daughter and sister. We also see that Nin uses the diary to pose practical and psychological questions of writing.

In *Volume One*, Nin further reflects on using the diary to expose the idiosyncrasy of the world a writer must navigate. She writes: "Writers do not live only one life, they live two. There is the living and then there is the writing. There is the second tasting, the delayed reaction" (1:73). The "tasting" of one's life that the writer engages, according to Nin, is inextricably linked to the cultural context and psychological reality in which one lives and writes. For example, in the later years of her life, Nin describes writing, as enacted on the diary site, as a means of defeating personal infernos, and also a way of contacting the *prima materia*, the first matter for the alchemical magnum opus. Nin writes, "It became the diary of an adventurer. It made me look at my life, at sorrowful moments, at moments of great disintegrating experiences, and constantly reminded me that it was an adventure, that it was a tale" (*A Woman Speaks* 157). Nin used the diary to gain narrative sense of herself within a "disintegrating" world. She relied on her diary to help transform disorder and restore faith in a perilous world. The diary, insofar as it encircles the unfolding of multiple selves, and forms cosmos, as well as explores the link between art and life, has a close relationship with myth. As a genre, the diary validates the making of the myth of the diarist in its heroic graciousness; therefore, it is time to examine the trickster/trickstar archetype in relation to the myth of the diarist.

As the diarist is engulfed in her own writing, derived from an instinctual nature to know the faces of reality, the physical diary categorizes a re-joining of the world around her. Therefore, the link between narrating her life story (myths) in a menacing world as a process of invention and discovery is intimately allied with an ability to "tell all the truth but tell it slant," as captured in the opening line of Emily Dickinson's poem.[1] Nin, as well as Dickinson, was ambivalent about truth; be it too "blinding" or too open-ended, truth is best told with a "slant." Consequently, Nin knew that writing about one's life (personal myth) compels one to rely on the combination of myths, imagination in its polyvocal qualities, memories and strong emotions, which make up a mythopoesis, rather than a strictly literal truth.

At play in the myth of the diarist, in the way in which the genre has the ability to hold the open-ended nature of truth through a plural subjectivity, and concern for ways of the *mundus inversus* (inverted world), brings to mind the conditions in which the trickstar/trickster comes into being, as well as the inherent trickery and symbolic aspects of self-construction. The trickster, in mythology, is "about a consciousness developed in the context of an unreliable and sometimes threatening existence," as pointed out by Susan Rowland in *The Ecocritical Psyche: Literature, Evolutionary Complexity and Jung* (103). We meet the trickster through indirection, duality, slant and shadows; we meet the trickster on the road, often at crossroads. The trickster archetype is a boundary crosser as well as a boundary creator by revealing a dimension previously hidden (Hyde 7). James Hillman posits that archetypes "tend to be metaphors rather than things" and allow "psychological understanding at a collective level" (xiii). Archetypes are deep patterns of psychic functioning (Hillman xiii). In this way, archetypal psychology reminds us that literalism hardens the heart and prevents deeper structures of the imagination from being explored (149). James Hillman's, as well as C. G. Jung's, articulation of archetypes captures the essence of my use of the term archetypes. For Jung, the collective unconscious consists of archetypes that are embodied, and symbolic art "has its source not in the person unconscious of the poet, but in a sphere of unconscious mythology whose primordial images are the common heritage of mankind" (Jung 80). Thus, I use archetypes to mean the images from the unconscious that animate the individual and the collective, and they can be found in relics such as myth, literature (including literary diaries), films and pop cultural representations. My suggestion, then, is to characterize the myth of the diarist by framing it within the trickster archetype as a way to better understand the boundary play that exists in the diary as a literary genre. Marlene Kadar makes a similar point in her essay, "Coming to Terms: Life Writing – from Genre to Critical Practice," by describing autobiography and diaries as "a genre with the potential to cross boundaries and disciplines" (10). The boundary-crossing ability, and truth-telling capacity, is likened to the metaphor of the trickery possible when viewing a vessel containing water. The diary has the possibility of holding illusions as well as tricks.

This brings me to one of the central tensions surrounding Nin's work that preoccupied many of her critics surrounding a "truth claim," which questions authenticity and facts in her work. This unease concerns not only the truthfulness of Nin's diaries, but also the relationship between her diaries and her fiction. In her essay "Aesthetic Lies," Suzanne Nalbantian analyses the ways in which Nin's diaries reveal a struggle with "psychoanalyst's concepts of personal truths in contrast to her perception of the truth acquired through fiction" (11). Nin explored her artistic sense of truth as is captured in this diary entry dated March 1933. Nin writes: "I always run away from the simplest phrases because they never contain all of the truth. To me, truth is something which cannot be told in a few words, and those who simplify the universe only reduce the expansion of its meaning" (1:73). What is more, Nin believed that if one "goes very far all values shift. It will not do to stay on the same ground forever. If you are terribly truthful, the ground will always move from under you, and you will have to shift with the constant shifting truth" (*D. H. Lawrence: An Unprofessional Study* 35). To develop her own understanding of selfhood, Nin explored the metaphor of a multifaceted self. Thus, a pivotal question is, at which crossroads do we encounter Nin? Nalbantian rightly posits that Nin can be found within an ambiguous territory that resides between fact and fiction, where for Nin, "life and art were mingled in an inextricable unity" (20). I propose we look for Nin at the intersection of three roads: where fact, fiction and myth reside. After all, Nin shares, "I am not a patient craftsman in writing. I like to keep the aliveness and the freshness of writing. I like the first spontaneous version, the explosion of seeds, the opening of new roads" (2:44). Here Nin's reference to "opening of new roads" is aptly reminiscent of where the trickster is located in ancient Greek mythology. The road the trickster travels is a spirit road, and it moves between heaven and earth while guiding souls (Hyde 6). Each diary entry, as it explores the "spontaneous versions" of a sense of self, holds the capacity to re-configure and explore a reality that links the trickster spirit to the diary. In addition, her diaries, created through the mythopoetic imagination, become a shared document that the community could then contemplate.

To be clear, I am not suggesting that Nin herself as a historical person is a trickster, for, as a woman, Nin is far more complex, and one archetype is not sufficient to cover the way Nin, or any diarist, writes her or his story. In addition, a comprehensive study of the trickster is indeed beyond the scope of this study; however, in this chapter I am interested in trailing trickster traits, expressed through creativity, which propel myth-making in the diary. Susan Rowland points out that, "Trickster myths remind us always of the chaotic, unpredictable, even indifferent qualities of living in the world" (Rowland 106). A mythic perspective, we should recall, presents "another vantage point, thereby placing us in two ontological spaces at once" (Hillman 159). I propose that we read Nin's diaries from these two mutually relating ontological spaces, the literary and the mythical.

Trickster narratives reflect and expose the prejudices, vulnerability and fragility of our social order. It is my hope that by exploring the trickster as an archetypal phenomenon, in conjunction with Nin's diaries, we could see that the diarist, at times, must be trickstar/trickster in her own instinctual nature to create as a way to endure. As a concept the trickstar/trickster evolves from folklore and mythological sources, which I will also explore further in this chapter. While the question of the proper myth of the diary remains multifaceted, I am curious: what is revealed when the trickstar/trickster archetype is seen sauntering along a parallel path in Nin's diaries? Ultimately, I argue that the trickstar/trickster qualities, used to construct a sense of her life story, reveal earth-mother consciousness being embraced in the literary diary.

Locating the trickstar/trickster in the navel of the earth

In *Volume Two* of her diary, one of Nin's celebrated descriptions of the act of writing is linked to a descent: "To write is to descend, to excavate," she declares (2:41). Nin describes the descent to one's inner life as having the mythic structure of the labyrinthine city "of Fez, with its Arabian Nights gentleness, tranquility and mystery" (235). What is found is not merely an ordinary voice, but rather a mythological voice that is excavated from the depths of the earth. The plunge to find one's mythological voice brings to mind Clarissa Pinkola-Estés's metaphor of the *rio abajo rio* (river below the river) as the psychic place where *la voz mitológica* (the mythological voice) resides. The river below the river is accessible through "deep meditation, dance, writing, painting, prayer-making, singing, drumming, active imagination" (Estés 27). Nin arrives at the river bank through her own courage, creative acts and ritual of diary writing.

Nin's link between the creative act of writing and a descent into the city of Fez is an allusion to *Arabian Nights*, also referred to as *One Thousand and One Nights*, recalling the folklore character and legend, Scheherazade. In the prologue of the stories, Scheherazade lives in a patriarchal wasteland, engaging in inventive deviations in her storytelling stratagems to twist the circumstances to her favor as a means of survival. Nin's fascination with Scheherazade as a fantasy persona is referenced when she dresses like Scheherazade to attend a masquerade: "I came as Scheherazade and told stories. I wore a nylon iridescent dress that seemed like water, and, as a headdress, a Christmas-tree ornament that looked like a fan, from which the water-like, floating, transparent texture fell like a waterfall" (5:140–141). The interchange between masquerading, transparency and truth-telling perpetually fascinated Nin. In her essay "Aesthetic Lies," Suzanne Nalbantian reflects on Nin's frequent public appearances in masquerade-like costumes and describes Nin's style as "simply theatrical." Nalbantian writes, "I remember most her eyes, covered with maquillage, which gave the impression of an actress's face" (16). Nin's own explanation of her costumes was that they were akin to masking, for "lies seem like a costume, small lies, deviations mostly" (*Incest Diary* 179). Even more compelling in Nin's allusion to Scheherazade is the circumstance in which Scheherazade comes to rely on tricks, when only a trick could help her stay alive, as she tells the folktales in *Arabian Nights*. What does Scheherazade's context in which she sets off on a voyage of storytelling imply about the myth of the diarist? What does the hostility Scheherazade faces reveal about the transformative possibilities of the diarist in the labyrinths of her own psyche? To explore these questions, it is necessary to return to the folktale *Arabian Nights*.

In the prologue to the *Arabian Nights* we learn that Scheherazade is the oldest daughter of the vizier who served King Shahraya. The king has been betrayed by his wife's infidelity; he is not alone, as it turns out, for his younger brother Shahzaman shares the same fate. In revenge, each brother drives a sword into his respective wife and her lover. When they are together, the brothers commiserate with one another on the betrayal they have suffered from women. King Shahraya decides that he must purge the whole country of those particularly dangerous and deceitful maidens suitable for marriage. He orders his vizier to deliver him a new bride each night with whom he will presumably make love, but he really intends to slay her the following morning. Following several fatal commissions, Scheherazade requests to be the King's next intended bride. Scheherazade's strategy is that she will tell an endless stream of tales. With the help of her sister, Dinarzad, the two decide Dinarzad will appear in the room once the king has had his "pleasure" with Scheherazade and request a story while time passes as they await dawn. Scheherazade is extremely calculating in her telling of tales, such that when dawn reaches, her tale is incomplete, unfinished; thus the king, enthralled in her story, cannot kill her until he hears the complete tale. In this way, Scheherazade spends the thousand and one nights of storytelling, thus sparing her life. By the end, the king is soothed and transforms his anger towards the opposite sex. Furthermore, Shahraya better understands Scheherazade through her tales, realizing that the entire female gender is not genetically tainted. He learns to humanize women as unique individuals (Jurich XV). Scheherazade's story, among other themes, is not just about using trickery to stay alive, but gaining a voice to help heal the ills, violence and disenfranchisement committed by patriarchy. It is this context that reminds us that stories serve as more than mere entertainment. Pieced together night after night as in *Arabian Nights* – akin to daily diary entries – stories are a procession of patchwork. Each story and diary entry helps to avert the storyteller and her audience from being disoriented in a world filled with destruction and disillusionment, as well as serve to restore faith in oneself and to the community. The sentiment of writing and creating in a wasteland reverberates the patriarchal context in which Nin used her writing to seek and construct her own sense of selfhood.

Marilyn Jurich in her book, *Scheherazade's Sisters: Trickster Heroines and Their Stories in World Literature*, argues that upon close observation of the behavior of the male trickster, it is clear that females may also be considered tricksters. Thus, Jurich's nomenclature *trickstar* holds the characteristics of the male trickster as well, including the shape-shifting and gender-changing nature. I will later discuss the ways in which Hermes, the ancient Greek trickster, is paired with Hestia in art and literature. However, it is important to point out that in folklore the trickstar is a distinctive and vital female figure in the story that presides over possibility and shifts.

The title of Jurich's book *Scheherazade's Sisters: Trickster Heroines and Their Stories in World Literature* ties into her thesis that Scheherazade fits into the framework of a female trickster. Jurich introduces the nomenclature "trickstar" to describe specifically the female tricksters, for they "are 'stars' in trickery" (xiv). It is true that an entire catalogue can be used to define trickstar (yet I am reminded of the trickstar's propensity to disassemble and to escape constructs, as her presence is felt writing this chapter). Nonetheless, I include four archetypal traits in my analysis. Throughout her book, Jurich identifies many archetypal traits of the trickstar; however, the four characteristics primary to my analysis are: (1) in early folklore, the trickstar is a female- embodied character that carries a vital force as the protagonist controlling the narrative; thus, biological sex holds importance for the trickstar; (2) the trickstar is a twice-marginalized figure, making her both border-dweller and border-crosser; (3) she holds a plural subjectivity. Therefore, it is not surprising that the trickstar, in order to include all aspects of her experiences, and by knowing the limitations in the social norms in which she operates, uses alternative strategies, and personas, to attain a goal, which can include creating narratives from her own subject position. I add to this trait the resulting juxtaposition of initiator/creator in the female trickster. This is a way for the trickstar to hold a multitude of instincts and experiences; (4) she holds erotic and relational aspects that can make her a seducer; here I expound that as seeker, she can stir up cultural constructs by, oftentimes, committing unsociable acts as a way to develop her cultural milieu. In this case, she is likened to another juxtaposition: seducer/seeker. In times like this, her strength as shaper of societies, often as a seducer, reflects her experiences as a twice-marginalized figure (Jurich 3–20). While the consequences and associations between tricks and women have been traditionally regarded with a mixture of suspicion and awe in folklore, according to Jurich's research, it is true that female writers, such as Nin, have suffered under the double bind of their gender, as I have noted throughout this study.

An early manifestation of the trickstar can be seen in an Albanian folktale, *The Tricks of Women and Other Albanian Tales*, collected by Paul Fenimore Cooper and published in 1929. The short story "The Tricks of Women," worth repeating here, persuades the reader about the ways of women that keep them from being discovered by members of the opposite sex (Jurich 1). The story is about a young man who decides he will not marry until he knows all there is to know about women. He sets out on a journey and along the way engages with many women, and he records his findings on women's tricks. With a boastful attitude, assuming he has learned all there is to know about women, he approaches the king to share his findings. The queen is determined to "expose his hubris" and while the king is away one night, the queen snuggles up next to the boy. He thinks she is making a sexual advance, and he is prepared to respond through sensual touch. The queen cries out to the king's servant. The queen covers for him, explaining, "this poor dear boy was eating, a bone stuck in his throat and he nearly died" (Cooper 34). The boy, out of his own curiosity, corroborates with her story. Here we see the queen use her body through seductive jesters to crush the boy's understanding of his own expertise in the ways of women, revealing that the boy's sense of understanding of women is wholly inadequate. In the end, the queen advises the boy, "The tricks of women aren't to be learned. You go back home and marry and be like everybody else, because not even the devil has learned the tricks of women" (Cooper 36).

The queen's final statement raises a connection to women's spite outsmarting the archetype of evil in Christian cultures (Jurich 2). Moreover, the association of women, seduction and tricks, as revealed in this tale, point to the notion that the nature of trickster is then substantially intensified in the dealings of the female trickster, the trickstar (Jurich 3). The trickstar has the propensity to confuse her audience, shock, amuse and inspire as she contrives her way out of confining, even life-threatening circumstances (Jurich 3). This tradition, however, is supported by patriarchal cultures and more often than not prefers to see the trickstar as menacing, and her tricks as merely self-serving (3). Consequently, to better understand the trickstar, one must realize that since women have been marginalized and disempowered in so many areas of our culture for so many centuries, the tricks of women will be unlike the tricks of men. As a female Modernist writer, both embracing and creating the myths of the time, the marginalization Nin experienced, including her exploration of sexuality, plurality of subjectivity, and seduction, took form in her diaries with intricate traces of the trickstar archetype.

The Albanian Queen, like Scheherazade, knows that in some situations, only a trick could burgeon. While the Queen resorts to trickery to expose hubris, Scheherazade's trickery escapes violence from the King. In a skillful way, Scheherazade, very much a trickstar, gauges the timing of the plot of her story along with the appropriate inflection (Jurich xiv). Scheherazade knows that "power must be tricked out of power, and the powerless have only the trick as their resource," writes Jurich (xvii). Scheherazade learns to embody her stories by becoming mindful of her breath, gesture, facial expression, hand and body movements until the next day, when she must trick the king into sparing her life one more night (ibid xiv). Hence, we are reminded that the art of storytelling is both archetypal and physical, and that the body is connected to the imaginal psyche. The trickstar is one who slyly conceals her motives and gauges her actions to effect transformation (ibid xvii).

In effect, Nin explains that the context for writing in the early diary was a "habit which [she] acquired accidentally as the result of a psychic trauma" (*A Woman Speaks* 157). Yet the initial context, or "color," shifts from one diary volume to another. Nin tells this openly when she writes that the diary "[became] a guiding element in life and took on a different color after a while" (*A Woman Speaks* 157). The impetus of Nin's early diary, however, dates to 1914 when Nin's father, Cuban-born Joaquin Nin, abandoned the entire family. This forced separation was traumatic for Nin. Indeed, the year 1914 coincided with the beginning of a collective catastrophe for all those who were affected by the mammoth tragedies of World War I. Nin's mother, Rosa Culmell, also Cuban-born, like countless other families escaping the traumas of war, brought her family to America to begin a new life. The physical journey Nin embarked upon along with her family, from Barcelona to New York, began an intricate and extended mythic voyage into her sense of self that is courageously recorded in her diary, *Linotte* 1914–1920. On July 25, 1914, Nin, 11 years old, begins her diary with the following entry: "Last look at Barcelona and last thoughts. The mountains rise up in majestic beauty. The setting sun shows its last pale rays. Here and there, the blue sky holds little white clouds. As I look at this landscape, my mind is crowded with thoughts. We are going to leave Barcelona, leave this beautiful country" (*Linotte* 3). In a new country, Nin would be forced to bridge various cultural frontiers, activating a trickster archetype. She developed an English-speaking identity alongside her Spanish and French identities. This triadic personality learned to juggle cultural identities, as she would never again be merely one person navigating one culture. Traveling in an unknown land on a new continent is similar to the discovery of an unfolding personal mythology. In *Anaïs Nin Observed: From a Film Portrait of a Woman as Artist*, she writes, "It started as a letter to my father and ended as a letter to the world. And now it's a correspondence – communion with the world" (Snyder 20). In essence, initially, Nin used the "stories" in her diary both to distract herself from confusion and chaos of a war-stricken world, and also to distract her father from the time that had passed since their separation. Nin also attempts to disclose herself to her father so that he may better get to know her. Just as Scheherazade was concerned with revealing herself to the King so that he might know her personal world, Nin, too, used storytelling, charm and seduction in her diary in hopes of bridging the gap with her absent father.

Before turning to the role of charm and seduction in Nin's diaries, it is important to understand that much space in the diary is devoted to play, specifically the playing of multiple roles (Podnieks 65). James Hillman, writing about archetypal psychology in his book *Re-visioning Psychology*, argues that "the archetypal perspective provides a common connection between what goes on in any individual soul and what goes on in all people in all places in all times" (xiv). To speak of archetypes, then, one must note the plurality involved when considering that points of view toward any psychological event represent the many-sidedness of human nature, including the variety of viewpoints experienced by one individual. Nin's diary reveals a struggle with this psychological notion when she notes: "How difficult it is to be 'sincere' when each moment I must choose between five or six souls. Sincere according to which one, reconciled to which one?" (1:118). The polyvocal texture of Nin's diary can be better understood from the point of view of archetypal psychology, as Nin through her diary explored the many facets of her identity. In her diary Nin admits this complexity when she writes, "Always imagining another role. Never static"(2:26). Another essential point James Hillman contributes to our understanding of literary diaries is that from an archetypal stance, psychic reality is "not 'I,' but we; not one, but many. Not monotheistic consciousness looking down from its mountain, but polytheistic consciousness wandering all over the place" (Hillman 33). The mercurial aspect of the creative polytheistic psyche is what Nin was drawn to recording and representing in her diary. Likewise, the link between diaries and their construction of complex identities can also be considered in terms of Domna Stanton's suggestion that the diary is a literary space where the diarist not only explores the conflicting roles within a patriarchal order, and the desire for a creative selfhood, as in Nin's case, but similarly informs the complex construction of a new mythology to live by. Now, another question is: what is the role of charm and seduction in Nin's personal myth, from an archetypal perspective? It is to an analysis of the archetypal function of seduction and charm in Nin's diaries, particularly *Volumes One* and *Two*, that I turn to next.

Tricks through charm and seduction

Reflecting on the matter of women, resources and trickery, Jurich reminds us that for the most part, women historically have not had the possibility of bargaining with money or status, and cannot promise political alliances in exchange for larger individual pursuits. Therefore, often women's negotiating power must "depend on rousing fear or desire in the unwary 'trader,' the person to whom she must appeal in order to get freedom of action or be released from confinement" (19). Mostly, the trickstar relies on her cunning, erotic attraction and brain-power. For example, Scheherazade as a trickstar archetype decides on the most appropriate trick, and what better than the fragment of a story as a delaying tactic to please the king in order to spare her life? It appears that only the trickstar could instruct in an imaginative way that includes gesture, an embodied voice, and sensuous promise. Scheherazade uses her female charm, along with well-thought-out stratagems to exterminate the King's fear, distrust, dangerously fitful behavior and harmful ideologies about gender. It is through her well-crafted plan that she restores faith and transforms values (Jurich xiv–xv).

Surely, seduction and language is a dynamic in Nin's work, as has been noted by critic Helen Tookey in her book *Anaïs Nin, Fictionality and Femininity: Playing a Thousand Roles*. Tookey references a revealing diary entry dated in the Fall of 1957, *Volume Six*, in which Nin reflects on the past associations between writing, seduction and her father. Nin writes:

> Every act related to my writing was connected in me with an act of charm, seduction of my father. Every act was accompanied by guilt and retraction. Every act was doomed. I was doomed by the enormity of my sin (the wish to charm my father) to be punished, to fail. Every act from selling a book, accepting a dollar, involving others, was charged with direct sexual associations: courting the world. In my dreams I did not publish *Under a Glass Bell* but I bought a vulgar parrot-green dress, a whorish dress. In my dreams at night I did not achieve a work of art and present the world with it, but I lay naked on a bed (with an invisible lover) and all the world could see me.
>
> (6:109)

Nin reflects on the way that her writing began as interrelated with remorseful and sexual (Oedipal) associations with her world. As mentioned earlier in this chapter, the impetus for Nin's early writing was a strong emotional desire to reconnect with her long-absent father. It was through her writing that she exposed herself, feeling sexual and shameful. Moreover, Tookey links Nin's open engagement with seduction and interest with the actress, to Nin's fascination with the *femme fatale*; the beautiful but deadly fatal woman is personified above all as exotic, as alluring and at times as the embodiment of evil. She can be both a passive and dependent creature. Tookey argues that for Nin, "the figure of the actress takes center stage as the quintessentially Modernist (patriarchal) fantasy of the feminine" (91). A historical perspective of the discourse of the feminine is found in the *femme fatale*, as noted here:

> The figure of the femme fatale represents the point of convergence of various key discourses of the late nineteenth and early twentieth centuries, including urban modernity, psychoanalysis, and the "society of the spectacle." Above all, the femme fatale is a focus for anxieties about both female sexuality and the stability of the self. The former anxiety was particularly bound up with the discourses and experiences of modern urbanization and consumerism (the "streetwalker-princes" figure of "La Parisienne"); the latter, with psychoanalysis.
>
> (Tookey 108)

The *femme fatale* holds the anxiety of a culture coping with what it means to meander an unreliable world through secretiveness, deception and a kind of anti-knowledge, as it would have been considered in the late 19th century (Tookey 108). Traces of the trickstar spirit run through the literary veins of the *femme fatale*, for she represents the chaotic and unpredictable qualities of self-representation.

Consequently, Tookey points out, Nin's preoccupation with the actress, "the duplicitous, role-playing woman," and the *femme fatale* – "seductive and problematic fantasies of the feminine" – recur in Nin's short story "Sabina." This short story is transmogrified from *Volume One* of Nin's diaries dating from 1931 to 1934, including an account of Nin's relationship with June Miller (108). According to Tookey, the recurring image of the veil in the story, as well as throughout Nin's work, suggests the role of simultaneously concealing, revealing and provoking (108). Tookey sees the veil as symbolic of a bodily and sexual tease. The tension between concealing and revealing that Tookey convincingly points to has a connection to the *femme fatale*. What is important to point out here is that from an archetypal assessment, the *femme fatale* resembles a flattening of Aphrodite in her modernity. In her study of Aphrodite in *Pagan Meditations: Aphrodite, Hestia, Artemis*, Ginette Paris maintains that in the realm of the double standard of sexual morality and expression, the connection to Aphrodite as urging and concealing truth is a way to avert male domination (Paris 64). What is more, the veil for Aphrodite is symbolic of the problem of truth-telling, for when immersed in a "multivalent reality," it is difficult to express anything "truly monovalent" (Paris 65). In Nin's life, meandering male domination was a common theme; therefore, it is unsurprising that throughout her life she was dedicated to understanding creative ways to navigate the duplicitous waters, and ultimately transcend the confines of patriarchy. Nin admitted in the Diary: "The veil was sundered, and soon after, I covered the truth again. Eddies of illusion engulf reality again. I have accepted a self which is unlimited" (1:200). Thus, it is up to the reader to intuitively know that in the erotic, sometimes veiled, and mercurial world of Aphrodite, resorting to seduction and tricks is often inescapably at play.

Tookey's reference to Nancy Scholar's work in "Autobiography as Seduction" seems to offer a one-dimensional reading of Nin's seductive world. Scholar, Tookey notes, posits that "Nin's mythic self-construction and 'revelations' in the diaries must be seen as an extended striptease, directed ultimately at the seduction of the father, and more generally at the seduction of all her readers, who may be taken as standing in for the father" (118). Tookey seems to agree that Nin's experience with seduction, men and writing revolves around a prevailing desire to please men, particularly her father. While this interpretation seems to capture Nin's early life experiences, it does not illuminate Nin's continual lifelong exploration of the intricacies of living and creating a language to depict what it is like to be in a "multivalent reality." Tookey also lends consideration to Nin's identification with seduction, language and the actress by considering Diane Richard-Allerdyce's insightful interpretation in *Anaïs Nin and the Remaking of Self: Gender, Modernism, and Narrative Identity*. Richard-Allerdyce argues that central to Nin's work is her preoccupation with playing the role of inventor and creator of her own life as a lifelong attempt to recover from the deep wounds of emotional, and possibly sexual, abuse she experiences from her father (Richard-Allerdyce 45). Indeed, Nin, the diarist as artist, explores an at times disintegrating world of duality and distortions through the juxtaposition of seducer/seeker necessary to her art, and at times, existence. What is more, Nin uses her creativity to reorder past trauma as a way to develop her craft, and to then create a narrative independent of her father. For me, this latter interpretation sheds light on Nin, the diarist, creating a world in which she could construct regardless of whether it required her to break social norms. As she was engulfed in her writing – in love with creating – being propelled by a psychic instinct to know, to integrate experiences, Nin created a feminine art form of her own through risks and tricks.

Trickstar: Inanna and the god of wisdom

To further explore the mythic motif of disrupting the social order to transform cultural constructs, let us turn to Inanna in the Sumerian myth "Inanna and the God of Wisdom." By considering the archetypal role of a trickstar as shaper of society, I propose we gain another ontological position, broadening the perspective of art created by a feminine imagination such as that of Anaïs Nin. Through a close look at the Inanna myth, we learn of a pattern of behavior within confining social conditions.

The myth of Inanna is an ancient Sumerian myth that centers on a woman as goddess and queen, possibly dating to pre-patriarchal society. Although the myth hints at the possibility of male constructs of women's roles in a patriarchal society, I want to underscore that my curiosity about this myth is tied to its relationship to the myth of the diarist, based on its archetypal essence, as noted earlier in this chapter. "Inanna and the God of Wisdom" is known to be a myth about the transfer of the arts of civilization from the neighboring kingdom of Eridu to Uruk, Inanna's own queendom. In this myth, Inanna ventures out to test her powers, eager to be "fertilized," and commits unsociable actions that alter the depths of her life and overall her cultural milieu. Unlike the hero wielding the all-powerful sword as he sets out on a journey, Inanna instead relishes her sexuality. She demonstrates vitality and strength as she sets out to test her influence. In the myth, we are told that Inanna:

> placed the shugurra, the crown of the steppe, on her head.
> She went to the sheepfold, to the shepherd.
> She leaned back against the apple tree.
> When she leaned against the apple tree, her vulva was wondrous to behold.
> Rejoicing at her wondrous vulva, the young woman Inanna applauded Herself.
>
> (Wolkstein 12)

By adorning herself with the crown, Inanna prepares herself to play the role of Queen. For once the crown of the steppe is in place, the performance begins.

She leans against the apple tree delighting in her strength gained from her embodiment – her wondrous vulva. Then she sets off for the sheepfold, which is the center of nature in Sumer. The words sheepfold, womb, vulva, loins and lap are all synonymous in Sumerian and are images linked to fertility (Wolkstein 146). The basic plot of the myth reveals that Inanna embarks by boat, alone to visit Enki in Eridu, the God of Wisdom and the Water – to be "fertilized" by "the sexual as well as the magical, spiritual, and cultural powers of life – both for herself and for her queendom" (Wolkstein 147). Inanna sets out with a wondrous vulva, as she flaunts (seduces) and celebrates her feminine vitality, sexuality and fertility. In the epithets Inanna is referred to as "daughter," "maiden," "womanly," giving her a metaphoric father-daughter identification. As far as Enki's identity, he is the God of Water and the God of Wisdom. As God of the Waters, Enki is the fertilizer of the land, and organizer of his creation (Wolkstein 147). His iconographic emblem is the goat-fish, connecting him to the earth and water (Wolkstein 147). Importantly, "water" is the same word for "semen" in Sumerian (Wolkstein 139). In this way, Enki metaphysically is linked to wisdom and sexuality, including what is conscious and unconscious in psyche.

When Inanna arrives, Enki welcomes her as an intimate equal and the two of them rejoice in eating and drinking. Enki, "swaying with drink," toasted Inanna as "my daughter," and in his intoxication and over-confidence, 14 times he gives all of the *me*, "attributes of civilization," to Inanna, and 14 times Inanna accepted the holy *me* (Wolkstein 147). The *me* consists of over one hundred listings, and the "last six groupings, beginning with 'the art of the hero,' are related to humanity's concerns: political power, the secure dwelling place, crafts, husbandry, emotions, the family, counseling, and decision" (Wolkstein 147). While the *me* emphasizes the power of the priesthood and "servitude," the initiative Inanna demonstrates to actually take the *me* is pivotal to governing her own kingdom, and her own narrative (Wolkstein 146). So as Enki bestows the *me*, Inanna does not question the generous gift. Full of intention, before Enki wakes from a sinuous state, Inanna loads all the *me* on the Boat of Heaven. While it is unclear whether Inanna predicted the result of the drinking bout, or whether she simply seized the opportunity that presented itself, she demonstrates the keenly alert mind characteristic of the trickstar, as she decides to accept and keep the *me*.[2] Also bearing in mind Inanna as a trickstar, Marilyn Jurich, in *Scheherazade's Sisters: Trickster Heroines and Their Stories in World Literature*, understands her action of managing to persuade Enki to release the precious *me* as a gesture towards working for harmony and unity between their respective communities. Moreover, Inanna, trickstar-like, is a shaper of society, for she does not merely yield the existing *me*, but adds several new *me* that influence and change the lives of the people of Uruk:

> Then more *me* appeared – more *me* than Enki had given Inanna.
> And these, too, were announced,
> And these, too were presented to the people of Uruk:
> Inanna brought the *me*:

She brought the placing of the garment on the ground.
She brought the allure.
She brought the art of women.
She brought the perfect execution of the *me*. (26)

Inanna alters the social norms because she is seen as possessing genius and power, as Enki decides that his finest option is to ally himself with her. In the end, Inanna increases justice and creativity and thus contributes to the redistribution of power in Sumer (Jurich 213). However, before refurbishing her community with the new *me*, and thus influencing a changing society, Inanna must first overcome some obstacles. When Enki sobers up and realizes he has given all the *me* to Inanna, he sends his servant Ismud to recover it. To help her triumph through this pursuit, Inanna summons her inner spiritual sources, her *sukkal*, Ninshubur, who performs the role of an inner spiritual resource. Ninshubur defeats Enki's "monsters."

In this myth, the goddess Inanna, in trickstar form, makes visible a possible psychic vitality that can be interrelated to the inception of Nin's early experiences with language, and her deep desire to be an artist, as discussed earlier. In particular, Nin had an ardent desire to give a voice to her own narratives exploring untamed libido, a cultural taboo at the time. We know that Nin was propelled by a celebration of her feminine ability to transform diary writing by creating a language to narrate an intimate life story. Just as Inanna sets off to have her feminine powers tested, joins forces with more spiritual resources and emerges as a fuller woman, so too does Nin follow similar archetypal stages of understanding while transforming self, as recorded in her diaries. Likewise, Inanna's identification with her sexuality in exchange for agency reflects a role as a trickstar and thus a shaper of culture. It must be underscored that for Nin, to be initiator/creator within a patriarchal world posed a great dilemma that only she could resolve within the "private" space of the diary. What Nin recorded in her diary would eventually contribute to changing her cultural milieu.

Nin's extensive opus, created and written throughout her lifetime, can be seen as spiritual illumination that impelled her throughout her life – as well as the lineage of women that she left behind. Referencing the 1960s, Suzette Henke writes that Nin appeared as a "literary guru that appealed not only to the burgeoning flower child of that era but to women everywhere searching for revised subject-positions in the modern world" (119). In a reflection of her recollections of Nin, her longtime friend, the critic Bettina Knapp, writes, "Firm in her goals, authentic in her approach to people – is it any wonder that a coterie of admirers revolved around her? Anaïs joyed in helping others, as if she were fulfilling a very special act of destiny" (39). Like Inanna, Nin was zealous to test her feminine powers, willing to be "fertilized," and throughout her life, she was tested by a haunting past. This theme of using her inner spiritual sources to overcome darkness is also prevalent in Nin's work; for throughout her life, Nin clung to her diary as a spiritual source, as her *sukkal*.

Conclusion: Hermes, Hestia and the myth of the diarist

The link between poesies and language in Nin's literary dairies converge through a strong mythic force. It is at the juncture of language and the hermeneutic where Hermes, the ancient Greek trickster, God of communication and travel, animates the myth of the diarist. As an active mediator of creativity, he is often linked with one who brings about culture. In his essay "Inclusive Conclusion: Trickster – Met Players and Revealers," William J. Hynes reminds us that Hermes is associated with "activities that center upon human creativity: bringing of culture, laughter, business transactions, as well as opening of the doors of perception" (213). He also notes that while our culture encourages us to privilege order/logos as our commonality, "Tricksters argue that the common trait is creativity: imagination, invention, and experimentation" (213).

Also noteworthy is that Hermes is paired with Hestia in the *Homeric Hymn to Hestia* as the opposite of Hestia, for he is perpetually on the move in an unreliable world, making him amenable to change (Paris 181). The Hermes-Hestia mythic energy reminds us that mischievousness, and the truth-telling that involves a slant, is best captured and recorded in the literary diary – in Hestia's hearth. As pointed out in Chapter 1, Hestia is evoked in the space of the diary as a hearth of a multifaceted subjectivity.

Moreover, Hermes constellates creative consciousness in his role as an agent of creativity who transcends the constrictions of monoculturality (Hynes 212). William J. Hynes marvelously states:

> Beyond all mere "scouting out" of possible alternate personal or social constructs, the trickster reminds us that every construct is constructed. Not only is someone not confined to a single construct or style of order, she is not confined to a choice among alternative constructs. The hermeneutic puts us in contact with the sources of creativity from which we can be empowered to construct our own construct. The trickster's constant chattering and antics remind us that life is endlessly narrative, prolific and open-ended.
>
> (212)

It is in a creative state of perpetual narrative, "prolific and open-ended," that Nin lived her life; for her, as mentioned at the opening of this chapter, life was akin to an "epilogue, an unfinished book" (*Linotte* 251). The trickstar, as earth-mother consciousness, energizes Nin's psyche to develop and construct a sense of selfhood to reconnoiter social alternatives for her as well as for others.

At the end of *Volume Six*, Nin reflects on her preoccupation with transforming art, and specifically the genre of self-life writing, while struggling against patriarchy. She reveals the profound connection between creativity, courage and life. Nin writes:

> Perhaps it is a greater agony to live this life in which my awareness makes a thousand revolutions while others make only one. My span may seem smaller

> but it is really larger because it covers all the obscure routes of the soul and body seeking truth, seeking the antiserum against hate and war, never receiving medals for its courage. It is my thousand years of womanhood I am recording, a thousand women.
>
> (6:400)

With references to "revolutions," "medals" and "courage," Nin points out that World War II is a context for her diaristic stance, for Nin's response to war included advocating for social integrity through self-awareness. This passage also captures Nin, the artist, the shaper of society, reflecting on what it feels like to have tirelessly created and re-created consciousness. The concern with recording and capturing the "thousand years of womanhood" extends to *Volume Seven*. Nin writes "Where is Anaïs? . . . I cannot keep the same feeling after a thousand exchanges" (7:243). It is the "thousand exchanges" in life that Nin pursued in her art.

Notes

1 *The Poems of Emily Dickinson*. Ed. Ralph W. Franklin. Cambridge: Belknap Press of Harvard UP. 1951.

2 See Leana Wessels's article "An Analysis of the Extent to Which the Trickster Archetype can be Applied to the Goddess Inanna/Ishtar". Wessels looks at Inanna's actions and nature as characteristic of the trickster archetype.

Works cited

Cooper, Paul Fenimore. *The Tricks of Women and Other Albanian Tales*. New York: William Morrow and Company. 1927. Print.

Dickinson, Emily. "Tell All the Truth But Tell It Slant (1129)." *The Poems of Emily Dickinson*. Ed. Ralph W. Franklin. Cambridge: The Belknap Press of Harvard UP. 1951. Print.

Estes-Pinkola, Clarissa. *Women Who Run With the Wolves: Myths and Stories of the Wild Woman Archetype*. New York: Ballantine Books. 1992. Print.

Henke, Suzette. *Recollections of Anaïs Nin by Her Contemporaries*. Ed. Benjamin Franklin V. Athens: Ohio UP. 1996. Print.

Hillman, James. *Re-visioning Psychology*. New York: Harper & Row. 1975. Print.

Hinz, Evelyn J. Ed. *A Woman Speaks: The Lectures, Seminars, and Interviews of Anaïs Nin*. Chicago: Swallow Press. 1975. Print.

Hyde, Lewis. *Trickster Makes This World: Mischief, Myth, and Art*. New York: North Point Press. 1998. Print.

Hynes, William J. "Inconclusive Conclusion: Tricksters – Metaplayers and Revealers." *Mythical Trickster Figures: Contours, Contexts, and Criticism*. Eds. William J. Hynes, William G. Doty. Alabama: Tuscaloosa UP. 1993. Print.

Jung, C. G. (1969). *Memories, Dreams, Reflections*. New York: Random House. 1989. Print.

Jurich, Marilyn. *Scheherazade's Sisters: Trickster Heroines and Their Stories in World Literature*. Westport: Greenwood Press. 1998. Print.

Kadar, Marlene. "Coming to Terms: Life Writing – from Genre to Critical Practice." *Essays on Life Writing: From Genre to Critical Practice*. Toronto: Toronto UP. 1992. Print.

Knapp, Bettina L. *Anais Nin*. New York: Frederick Ungar Publishing. 1978. Print.

Nalbantian, Suzanne. "Aesthetic Lies." *Anaïs Nin: Literary Perspectives*. New York: St. Martin's Press. 1997. Print.

Nin, Anaïs. *D. H. Lawrence: An Unprofessional Study*. Chicago: Swallow Press. 1964. Print.

———. *The Diary of Anaïs Nin Volume One (1931–1934)*. New York: Harvest. 1969a. Print.

———. *The Diary of Anaïs Nin Volume Two (1934–1939)*. New York: Harvest. 1969b. Print.

———. *The Diary of Anaïs Nin Volume Five (1947–1955)*. New York: Harvest. 1969c. Print.

———. *The Diary of Anaïs Nin Volume Six (1955–1966)*. New York: Harvest. 1969d. Print.

———. *The Diary of Anaïs Nin Volume Seven (1966–1974)*. New York: Harvest. 1969e. Print.

———. *Linotte: The Early Diary of Anaïs Nin (1914–1920)*. New York: Harcourt Brace Jovanovich. 1978. Print.

———. *Incest: From A Journal of Love (1932–1934)*. New York: Harcourt Brace Jovanovich. 1992. Print.

Paris, Ginette. *Pagan Meditations: Aphrodite, Hestia, Artemis*. Dallas: Spring Publications. 1986. Print.

Podnieks, Elizabeth. *Daily Modernism: The Literary Diaries of Virginia Woolf, Antonia White, Elizabeth Smart, and Anaïs Nin*. London: McGill-Queen's UP. 2000. Print.

Richard-Allerdyce, Diane. *Anaïs Nin and the Remaking of Self: Gender, Modernism, and Narrative Identity*. Dekalb: Northern Illinois UP. 1998. Print.

Rowland, Susan. *The Ecocritical Psyche: Literature, Evolutionary Complexity and Jung*. New York: Routledge. 2012. Print.

Snyder, Robert. *Anaïs Nin Observed: From a Film Portrait of a Woman Artist*. Chicago: Swallow Press. 1976. Print.

Tookey, Helen. *Anaïs Nin, Fictionality and Femininity: Playing a Thousand Roles*. Oxford: Oxford UP. 2003. Print.

Wessels, Leana. "An Analysis of the Extent to Which the Trickster Archetype Can Be Applied to the Goddess Inanna/Ishtar." *Journal for Semitics* 22.1 (2013): 35–33. Project MUSE. Web. 11 November 2014.

Wolkstein, Diane and Samuel Noah Kramer. *Inanna: Queen of Heaven and Earth: Her Stories and Hymns from Sumer*. New York: Harper & Row. 1983. Print.

Chapter 4

(Un)veiling incest

The early diary of Anaïs Nin, Volume Four and *Incest: From a Journal of Love*

> Another great illusion that woman must use all her introspective clear-sightedness & unbiased bravery to destroy – for the sake of her *self respect* is the impurity of sex the realization in defiance of superstition that there is *nothing impure in sex* – except in the mental attitude to it – will constitute an incalculable & wider social regeneration than it is possible for our generation to imagine.
>
> (Mina Loy 1914)

As discussed earlier, Nin was committed to an exploration of the *mundus inversus* (inverted world) around her, in a style that was prone to metaphors. The years 1931–1934 were pivotal for Nin's developing creativity and emerging psychological viewpoints. At this time, while in her late 20s and early 30s, Nin was hard at work creating the space and language she needed within the experimental context of the time. As an artist, she was immersed in the works of Modernist writers such as Sherman Anderson, D. H. Lawrence, Marcel Proust, James Joyce, Gertrude Stein and Franz Kafka, and was reading Sigmund Freud, Carl Jung and Otto Rank. This chapter explores the ways in which the historical and cultural context of the 1920s and 1930s informs our understanding of Nin's novelette *House of Incest* alongside the posthumously published *The Early Diary: Volume Four, (1927–1931)* and *Incest: From a Journal of Love (1932–1934)*.

To move forward with her art, Nin was interested in exploring the folds that lie within psyche, embodiment and the imagination through a poetic language. To do so, she would rely on the metaphor of a costumed self. This meant that she would explore the imaginative ways that psychology engages with art. In a diary entry dated July 18, 1931, Nin reflects on the desire to be an analyst stemming from a discovery of her own "illness." Nin writes: "Analysis One: Symptoms: excessive irritability; excessive sensitiveness to noises; fears of all kinds, which I never felt before: of lightning, of being alone in the house, of walking alone in the city; excessive and inordinate anxiety and imaginings concerning those I love . . . All this is duly described by Freud and is called anxiety neurosis. Cause? Sexual" (*ED* 4:436). Nin seems to write the latter to please the analyst in her. Also, consistent with Freud's theory at the time, Nin considered that many of the tensions in her life and art were linked to psychological restlessness and trauma around sexuality. Nin then declared that what would "save" her would be an exploration of her own sexuality through "creation," and she would begin with the "desire of [her] dual nature, from the necessity [she] felt to be in love with Hugh and infatuated with someone else" (*ED* 4:436).[1] Moreover, Nin explored sexual and spiritual possibilities through a creative process that transmitted the costumed self of the writer.

In a diary entry in April 1930, Nin credits D. H. Lawrence for creating a world "to live in," contributing to her own creative, sexual and psychological awakening (*ED* 4:294). Nin was absorbed in the intellectualization and gathering of inspiration, and at this time she credits Lawrence's poetic language as providing the vision to pursue a "naturalness" in her own literary method. To move forward, Nin would rely on the juxtaposition of seducer and seeker linked to the female trickster, as discussed in Chapter 3. Nin found assurance enough for her own "loosened" tongue, and the breaking down of "reticence" she felt within herself. She knew, however, that the exploration of a plural subjectivity required "courage," as she would set out to transcend order and structure by at times embodying and depicting disorder. In 1932, Nin wrote her first book, *D. H. Lawrence: An Unprofessional Study*, which she began writing in April 1930.[2] While Lawrence had died two years earlier, his reputation of a sexual crusader endured. His novels were banned and caused scandals around the world. In her critique, Nin praises Lawrence for his ability to capture "entanglements in relations between men and women, between reality and unreality" while realizing "fantasies and life, are denied by most people" (*D. H. Lawrence* 31). Also, when considering homoerotic love, Nin found that Lawrence had a command of a praiseworthy "mystical attitude towards the flesh" (*D. H. Lawrence* 37). She links Lawrence's descriptions of bringing "the undercurrents of body and mind" to the literary surface, and credits Freud and Jung for doing the same. The only difference, according to Nin, was that Freud and Jung "are essentially scientists and they are read with the detachment and objectivity of scientific research" (*D. H. Lawrence* 32,33). In contrast, Nin believed that by transforming the psychological, including troubling and traumatic experiences, through the mythopoetic, one could, indeed, capture a sense of order, be it woven with fantasy. It was through the imagination that unrest and psychological sorrow could be given an expression. Nin writes: "But others know that the imagination is a constant deformer . . . But one experience can be multiplied by our imagination. And it is this power to multiply and to expand which creates at the same time intricacies and entanglements. Entanglements are the other face of the same activity" (*D. H. Lawrence* 32).

The "experience" and "entanglements" that Nin would work with creatively time and again in the coming years was the theme of emotional and spiritual obstructions linked to untamed libido. True to the trickstar spirit, it appears that Nin's imagination dwelled on the crossroads where "intricacies and entanglements" are found, wedded to life and death, and reimagined through her own mythopoesis. It is very clear that Nin's fascination and preoccupation with the obscurities and complexities of an intimate relationship with self as artist, and with others, was being unleashed. Nin's thematic focus of this time was symptomatic of larger cultural anxieties and concerns. It was in the social and cultural landscape of the late 1920s and 1930s that Nin was crafting a language in which to voice psychic pain, self-loathing, and spiritual and sexual discoveries, including an incest motif. Specifically, Nin's fascination with the symbolic treatment of homoerotic, lesbian love and incest was intensifying. At the time, Nin saw in the erotic a potential of self-contemplation to create a modern female self. She was compelled to explore the ways in which pursuing desire could lead to spiritual reclamation. Such audacity was most seen in the male realm of literature at the time. Sheri Benstock, in her book *Women of the Left Bank*, reminds us that "[a]lthough Nin refused to address the social and political issues of the 1930s directly, the psychopathology of the female spirit that is the subject of her writing in these years reflects a larger cultural paranoia and self-hatred" (435). Nin's protagonists, like Nin herself, fight against cultural constraints by "seeking integrity through self-awareness" (Benstock 435).

In her diary, on April 30, 1931 Nin records beginning a new prose-poem in a state of "fantasy-making," which she is hopeful could "fit in *transition*" (*ED* 4:424). It was in pursuit of "continuing the mood of the morning" in which she begins "pieces like bits of prose-poem" that happens to be the start of *House of Incest*. Nin moves on writing that she immediately "made a note on the psychoanalysis of the creator: creation by undirected imagining – a state of being like a trance – produces subconscious poetry" (*ED* 4:424). She reflects on the psychological source of the beginning of the prose-poem, as it is crucial to reference her aesthetic coherence of working with metaphorical incest images to construct a language for psychological terror and confusion. It should be noted that Nin's posthumously published *Incest: From a Journal of Love*, narrating an incestuous encounter with her father, is dated in 1933. Nin began writing *House of Incest* in 1931. Consequently, the fact that *House of Incest* begins two years before *Incest: From a Journal of Love* (1933) reveals Nin's early obsession with incest as a metaphor to explore the themes of self-love of the artist, and the creative and destructive potentials of an untamed libido. At the time, Nin celebrates having reached new shores in her creativity: "I'm entering a new phase in my writing" (*ED* 4:425). What follows this entry is a depiction of a cryptic house: "The house had the shape of an egg, and it was carpeted with cotton and windowless – one slept in the down and heard through the shell the street organ and the apple vendor who could not find the bell" (*ED* 4:425). This description referencing fertility, darkness and the underworld is the incestuous house in the novelette *House of Incest*. The mysteriously "windowless" house, set amid a wasteland in the backdrop, is symbolic of a psychic space wherein the narrator can probe all facets of her identity: "In the house of incest there was a room which could not be found, a room without window, the fortress of their love, a room without window where the mind and blood coalesced in a union without orgasm and rootless like those of fishes" (*House of Incest* 52). We are reminded that what Nin often brought into consciousness in her diary was plundered as raw material, and imaginatively explored in her fiction through a mythopoesis of her own.

The next month, Nin is emphatic about the discovery of a fresh direction in her writing. She declares having begun her "life's real work, the transposition of [her] Journal into a printable form" (*ED* 4:433). It seems, however, as if her new phase of diary writing includes a reassurance that in its capacity to hold the open-ended costumed self, her diary privileges another prominent juxtaposition linked to trickstar: initiator and creator of her own Modernist narrative. Nin evidently begins to experience her diary as a Modernist text. Emphasizing the influences of 20th-century Modernism had on Nin, Elizabeth Podnieks, in her book *Daily Modernism: the Literary Diaries of Virginia Woolf, Antonia White, Elizabeth Smart and Anaïs Nin*, writes that in the early 1930s, "Nin was constructing a persona for herself that would soon be identified with Freud. Her sense of self is an embodiment of his theories of a neurotic, fragmented psyche, which informed so much of modernism" (312). Indeed, Nin herself sees this "new phase" referring to both the writing in her diary, and fiction, to be in line with Modernism. She writes: "My modernism, so sincerely arrived at" (*ED* 4:464). Nin came to contextualize her literary works as contemporaneous with Modernism, especially in the use of insights into psychological turmoil, and mysticism as a literary technique, containing racy sexual content. Nin was exploring taboo topics in her *Incest: From A Journal of Love* at the time, which would be posthumously published nearly six decades after it was written. I turn to this diary later in this chapter. Also, it is in the backdrop of these unfolding years in the late 1920s and early 1930s that books containing what was considered scandalous content were banned, such as D. H. Lawrence's *Lady Chatterley's Lover* for its sexual content, published in 1929 in Paris and in the United States in 1960, following the famous obscenity trial; James Joyce's *Ulysses*, depicted masturbation and adultery, was published in Paris in 1922, but was in the spotlight for being banned in the United States until 1934. Also, Ernest Hemingway's *The Sun Also Rises*, in 1927, was being questioned for his use of words such as "bitch" and "balls" in the preparation for the novel's publication (Blume 181). Among other books being banned for sexual content was Henry Miller's *Tropic of Cancer*, published in Paris in 1934, and banned in the United States until 1964.

Nin began experimenting with her fiction early on, using an incest theme in her first novel *House of Incest* (1931). In this novel, the protagonist, in a perpetual state of solitude, probes her sense of identity as "two currents" rush through her. She believes that by pursuing her anima figure, she will be liberated from sorrowful memories as well as appease insistent self-loathing on one hand, and obsessive self-love on the other. Written in poetic prose, the plot is structured around seven parts. The story is framed by an image of the creative act birthed through the body: "The morning I got up to begin this book I coughed. Something was coming out of my throat: it was strangling me. I broke the thread which held it and yanked it out. I went back to bed and said: I have just spat out my heart" (11). The creative process is conceptualized as an object inside the body ("heart") that is then "spat" out. There are echoes of a shaman extricating pain from the body. Nin likens the artist with the shaman's capacity of eliciting the removal of pain to birth the creative "process" and to confirm the existence of the creation on the surface of the earth. This imagery reminds us that art, particularly during times of war or post-war, is birthed out of human affliction and vulnerability. What follows this passage is an evocation to the "instrument called the quena made of human bones. It owes its origin to the worship of an Indian for his mistress. When she died he made a flute out of her bones" (11). The quena is the traditional flute of the Andes, and in its composition of "human bones" of the deceased queen, evokes the motif of death and rebirth through art.

In the beginning of *House of Incest*, as if in the world of creation myth, the narrator associates herself with the fluid and creative waters of the origin of birth. Recollection, for the protagonist, is expansive as she claims to be "full of memories of the bells of the Atlantide" (15). This ancient place, Atlantide, is accessible through dreams and becomes a source of self-knowledge. The first four parts of the novel are dedicated to the narrator reaching into the depths of her memory, and she does so by evoking Mnemosyne, goddess of memory. It is, after all, Mnemosyne who enables her interior knowing to emerge, bringing forward the profundities of self that are caught in illusions and stagnant libido: "The muffled, close, half-talk of soft-fleshed women. The men she had embraced, and the women, all washing against the resonance of my memory" (22). In this sense, her libido is blocked and unable to flow outside of narcissistic love, toward renewal. What she seeks in this unusual metaphorical lesbian love is access to the inner roads leading to a more dynamic and integrated sense of self: "And she and I, we recognized each other; I her face and she my legend" (23). Here the metaphor of incest suggests the narcissistic self-love of an artist, which deeply preoccupied Nin's early years. The way Nin contended with this preoccupation is through her art, as seen in the opening image of this novel. The protagonist here strives to release a blocked libido amidst floating surrealist images of duality, communion with one and the same merging woman, insanity, costumes and Saturn, hoping to be appeased. The juxtaposing of beauty, love and horror, amusement and torture seem mimetic to the apocalyptic prediction prevalent in Europe in the 1930s. The references to "terror," "decapitated" landscapes and to "seeing more than is humanly bearable" resonate with a world ravished by war and excessive drive for power.

The subsequent form of incest love in part two of the story involves a sister's sexual desire for her brother: with "salted tears of defeat crystallized in the corners of her restless eyes," she declares: "I LOVE MY BROTHER!" (46). The narrator projects her own sex onto a male, animus figure. She desires his love and the world he inhabits and controls (Benstock 433). Followed by a declaration that she has kissed her brother's shadow, we learn that the impenetrable kiss of the silhouette on the real face "is like" the impossibility of their love to fuse. That is, the love of her own unconscious, that which lies out of her reach, cannot be joined between them.

The possibility of deviant relations within families as sexual perversion is also explored through the biblical image of "Lot and His Daughters," alluding to incest. The daughter is the object of patriarchal love, as Lot rests his hand "upon his daughter's breast while the city burnes behind them." They experience the "joy and terror of their love"; he experiences joy while the daughter experiences "fear racking her" (*House of Incest* 55). In this patriarchal world, pleasure and pain are intimately woven as neither of them, however, "cry of horror." The daughter, with her "costume tightly pressed around her so that her breasts heave and swell under his fingers," realizes the power she holds over her father. It is in this mythic universe that destructive forces, including psychic distress, and the exploration of cultural "expressions of that unease" can be reordered and redirected (Benstock 435). The reordering of cultural illustrations extends to religious rituals and context through the "modern Christ" image, which is central to the conclusion of the novel. The modern Christ was born skinless, making him relentlessly vulnerable to cruelty, anguish and distress in his surroundings. He suffers from "lash[es]" and "whips" of people's cruelty (69). It is because of the perpetual pain that he is unable to feel, thus denying him a human body in a material world. It is this Christ figure who speaks of incest as a metaphor: "If only we could all escape from this house of incest, where we only love ourselves in the other, if only I could save you all from yourselves" (70). What follows is a reference to dismemberment of androgynous bodies, as the incestuous relationship is transformed into an act of empowerment. Shari Benstock considers these images as a reminder that "culture itself is seen to be a destructive force that registers through art a violence against nature. Women's self-division and disfigurement are carved in 'the veined docile wood' of the living tree" (434). In this prose-poem, as Benstock points out, Nin traces "the effects of the societal consciousness on the individual mind, of the public on the private, of civilization on art, Nin rebelled against the cultural values of her time and cried out against the pervasive violence and aggression apparent in the world around her" (Benstock 345).

In the end of *House of Incest*, the dancer recovers from dismemberment, once she comprehends the meaning of her fantasies. Escaping blocked libido, she "dance[s] with the music and with the rhythm of earth's circle; she turned with the earth turning, like a disk, turning all faces to light and to darkness" (72). The dancer provides sensory confirmation of the experiences that at the start of the novel existed as mere interior knowledge. In a defaced landscape the dancer's body flickers "evenly, dancing towards daylight," as the narrator strives to be reborn amidst the archetypal image of dark earth in the daylight of consciousness, contrasting with the dream world (72). Nin too would strive to better comprehend the sense of torture, self-loathing and narcissistic love, as central to an incest motif throughout her early works. It would be through her exploration of these themes in her diaries and with Otto Rank in the unfolding years that Nin would better understand her creative drive in relation to the incest metaphor.

While Nin wrote *House of Incest* throughout the early 1930s, in March 1933, she claims to have written her novelette to "synchronize" with Artaud's "vision of the world" (1:188). In April 1931, she credits having been inspired by the French poet Arthur Rimbaud throughout the completion of the novelette (*ED* 4:422, 1:77). In a diary entry dated October 1933, Nin refers to *House of Incest* as "my season in hell" (1:289). She is referencing Rimbaud's poem *Season in Hell*, published in 1873. Both of these men, including Otto Rank, influenced the novel until its publication in 1936. What is more, Nin's exploration of her own awakening, in an intimacy with self through unchecked sexual desires, came at a time when intellectual dialogue between art and science were largely gripped by the Oedipus myth. Western society was pioneering attempts to bridge art and science, illuminating our understanding of erotica, sexuality, creativity and spirituality. Based on Nin's interests in what could be revealed by linking the novelist's and the psychoanalyst's polyphonic experiences through literature, she would have been familiar with the notion that unrestrained libido results in the destruction of a civilization, as depicted in the Oedipus myth. Consequently, she and her characters set out to discover and commune with self in the richness of a mythic and poetic backdrop.

Psychology, art and incest

While touched upon in Chapter 2, I now turn to briefly survey the intertwining psychological interests shaping Nin's milieu of the 1920s and 1930s. Some literary works do not need a context to be fully understood. However, often times, when polemic ensues, context is critical. Nin's posthumously published *Incest: From a Journal of Love* is one of those works. Without a comprehensive understanding of the milieu in which this diary was written, one could be left feeling steeped in bold emotions, merely questioning Nin's sexual exploits. The backdrop of this work is the emerging psychological theories, specifically centered around art, spirituality and sexual instinct, including incest and psychic trauma. This cultural context shaped Nin's own understanding and curiosity in the topics. Viennese physicians and others who were drawn to Sigmund Freud's (1856–1939) ideas met weekly for salons in Freud's apartment at Bergasse from 1906 until shortly after the start of World War I, in 1915.[3] In these discussions was included Otto Rank (1884–1939) (Rudnytsky xxii). By this time, Freud had defined his ideas on the Oedipus impulse and its role in psychological growth in *Interpretation of Dreams*, 1900, which he continued to develop into the Oedipus Complex throughout the period of 1908–1910 (Rudnytsky xxii). Importantly, it was during the first of these meetings that Otto Rank read the early inception of his work outlining the ideas he later develops in *The Incest Theme in Literature and Legend*. During the late 1920s and 1930s, Nin was immersed in incest theories written by Freud, Jung and Rank. As the subject of sexual instinct in relationship to the artist invaded Nin's psyche, she pioneered an exploration linking psychology and art from a female perspective, specifically evident in her unexpurgated, posthumously published diary *Incest: From A Journal of Love*, which I will discuss later.

During 1906–1912 Otto Rank similarly believed in Freudian psychology. Rank, however, placed emphasis on the relationship between the Oedipus impulse and the artist. A summary of Rank's thesis is: "The incest fantasy is simply the 'nuclear complex of neurosis' that 'dominates the unconscious psychic life of normal, determining their social and erotic orientation in life,' but is also 'of primary importance in the psychic life of the author'" (Rudnytsky xii). By 1912, while psychology was still a young discipline, the Oedipus complex was considered the hallmark of psychoanalytical truth with no other competing myth or explanatory paradigm (Rudnytsky xii). Also, a popular tendency at the time was for psychologists to project their own encounters with erotic transference onto their female clients, resulting in incestuous entanglements that were damaging to the women who were under their professional care.[4]

Otto Rank's belief that the incest complex resides at the root of the creative drive was of immense interest to Nin. In *The Incest Theme in Literature and Legend*, Rank reiterates his argument that "the incest complex with all its diversity, opposing aspects and derivatives represents the nuclear complex of neuroses and of the literary creative drive as well" (Rudnytsky XV). As for Nin, she pursued her own curiosity about the role that sexuality, fantasy, dream and creativity play in the psyche of the artist. This means that Rank's rising theories paint a clear connection as to why Nin was interested in his work, ultimately leading to their relationship beginning in November 1933. Although it is not likely that Nin would have read Rank's early works, as they were not all in translation at the time, it is likely that someone in her intellectual circle would have shared Rank's extensive thesis on incest motifs in literature with her.[5] By December 1932, however, Nin was fully engaged in reading Rank's work *Art and Artist*.[6] I will return to the profundity of this relationship shortly.

Famed psychoanalyst C. G. Jung (1875–1961) was among the triad ardently writing on the problems of libido and incest at this time. In 1912 both Jung and Rank published their works on incest: *Transformation and Symbols of the Libido*, by Jung, translated into English in 1916, and *The Incest Theme*, by Rank, translated into French in 1934. Both of these works underwent revision. For Rank the revisions spanned decades, through the 1930s, and for Jung his revisions lasted into the 1950s. Each revision reflected not only their respective authors' changing relationship with Freud, but also their increased interest in the subject of incest. In Jung's thinking, unlike in Freud's theory, incest was not literally related to the mother, but rather stemmed from a regressive movement of the libido (*Psychology of the Unconscious* 462). This means that for Freud, the Oedipus complex is a matter of fear of castration resulting in forbidden and repressed sexuality linked to a desire for the mother. This complex caused an ego/unconscious split. For Jung, however, the pre-Oedipal mother is related to the creative unconscious that works in concert to birth the ego. Thus, for Jung, it is both repressing, and plays a role in the forming of the ego/unconscious. Another distinction between Freud and Jung is in their views of libido. For Freud, it is sexual energy. In contrast, Jung considered libido to be neutral energy with both creative potential, including sexual or spiritual. Jung relates incestuous tendencies to "an adult who is psychologically incapable of linking his sexuality to its proper object" (*Analytical Psychology and Education*). What is more, the regressive libido, according to Jung at the time, is linked to the ability of the child to progress in thinking about "psychic conflict." In his second edition of "Psychic Conflicts in a Child," Jung writes:

> I also lay stress on the significance of thinking and the importance of concept-building for the solution of psychic conflicts. It should be sufficiently clear from what follows that the initial sexual interest strives only figuratively towards the development of thinking. Were this not so, the solution of the conflict could be reached solely through the attainment of a sexual goal, and not through the mediation of an intellectual concept.
>
> (*Development of Personality* 10, 11)

Jung points out that the child's incestuous longing does not involve a biological instinct, but is linked to the progress of thinking. This means that for Jung, incest images help propel the development of psyche. Here we can see Jung's interest in broadening the scope of the myth preoccupying Western consciousness, being that Freud's focused Oedipal myth had no rival at the time. In *The Ecocritical Psyche*, Susan Rowland reminds us that "Jung's pre-Oedipal (m)other is not an abyss of being, but rather an unconscious desiring to give birth to the ego. Hence the Jungian Oedipus complex has to be more of a co-operative partnership between (sky) father pulling the ego-hero away and (earth) mother willingly pushing the ego-hero away" (Rowland 34). Therefore, Jung's work would go on to focus less on sexual repression and infantile desires, and underscore the connection between the search for self as represented in metaphors and images found in mythology and his own theories (Rowland 27).

At the time that Jung was putting his theory forward, he knew his relationship with Freud was at risk. In *Memories, Dreams and Reflections*, Jung reflects on having to choose between his theory or his mentor: "When I was working on my book about the libido and approaching the end of the chapter 'The Sacrifice,' I knew in advance that its publication would cost me my friendship with Freud" (167). It was Jung's adamant belief that "incest signified a personal complication only in the rarest cases. Usually incest has a highly religious aspect, for which reason the incest theme plays a decisive part in almost all cosmogonies and in numerous myths. But Freud clung to the literal interpretation of it and could not grasp the spiritual significance of incest as a symbol" (167). Jung insisted on shifting the emphasis from the literal interpretations of incest to the mother's womb to that of a symbolic yearning for rebirth, including a spiritual awakening.

Jung, like Nin, sees the womb as the symbolic origin of creativity and as a way to help balance the over-valuing of masculinity at the time. For Nin, the womb is the center of creativity, holding "secrets" and "labyrinths," as I describe in Chapter 2. Also, it is important to note that Nin was keenly aware of Jung's evolving theory on the symbolism of incest. Nin would come to agree with Jung that incestuous desires do not always express themselves in literal incestuous relations. Rather, Nin's early works sought to explore the images and metaphors that could advance her fluid sense of self as an artist, pioneering a creative expression amidst the oppressive patriarchal structures at the time. In a diary entry dated November 27, 1932, in her posthumously published *Incest: From a Journal of Love*, Nin writes:

> A thoroughly neurotic book including all the symptoms, phenomena, descriptions of moods, dreams, insanities, phobias, manias, hallucinations – tableau of disintegration, *franker* than Lawrence's treatment of homosexuality . . . a reflection of Jung's attitude against Freud's – if we could understand the significance of the sexual symbol we would have the key to vast pregnancies and abortions, fecundations and impotences – *from* the sexual root, the imaginary world – as, for instance, incest does not mean only possession of the mother or sister – womb of woman – but also of the church, the earth, nature . . . The gesture is only a symbol with enormous significance (you can even taste of death in copulation).
>
> (*Incest* 52)

This impassioned passage reads as an epiphany where Nin is coming to terms with the connection between incest as a metaphor for "possession" as related to the expression of experiences with oppressive systems that, she contends, dominated all facets of a woman's existence. She understands the ways that Freud's and Jung's attitudes toward incest diverged, recognizing her alignment with Jung's impression of the creative flexibility found in incest metaphors. The "neurotic book" that Nin references seems to be *House of Incest*. Nin's interest in the psychology of the artist persisted and it is in her *Incest: From a Journal of Love* that she captures a woman lost in a fantasy world prone to metaphors that mediate between reverie and reality.

What if Nin had done more than just ardently read Jung's work? What if she had officially consulted with him, or even a Jungian psychotherapist? If so, on the one hand, perhaps his emphasis on psyche and the archetypal would have further vindicated Nin's own forging interests in the archetypal as a direct expression of the personal, including creativity. It is possible that Jung's belief in the need for a Western creation myth to embrace creative fluidity between libido, spirituality and art would have helped Nin maintain what she so vividly knew: that the archetypal structures contained in myth could represent the psychological realities of personal experiences. And Nin too, like Jung, knew that a culture saturated with masculine images, including the over-valuing of masculinization, led to psychic imbalance and gender inequality. Then again, Jung's emphasis on the prominent role that women played as men's anima and creative muse, which was already woven into Nin's struggles with finding her own strength in a world seeped in patriarchal double standards, would have deepened the burden she sought to undo.

While Nin did not consult with Jung in person, in April 1932, as noted earlier, Nin began her patient-therapist relationship with Dr. René Allendy, a psychologist to whom she was introduced by her cousin Eduardo. During a session with Allendy, Nin recounted giving herself pleasure and the sense of guilt that followed. She sought to delve beneath the conservative Catholic attitudes toward sex and female erotic life. She also confessed that she was not having orgasms. She writes: "I feel an imperative need to tell him my biggest secret: In the sexual act, I don't always experience an orgasm" (*HJ:* 172). Nin interprets her need to retell events she has so far kept to herself as an attempt at "piecing the fragments together," a theme which becomes critical to Nin's ideas about sexuality, self and writing, as first explored in her diary (*HJ:* 173). Nin, we are reminded, uses her diary as a space to gain a sense of her "multiplicity" of selves. In the latter passage, in straightforward prose, Nin reveals a previously guarded experience that would have been deemed socially inappropriate for a woman to express. This candid style can be appreciated by recalling Podnieks's argument that the diary is where Nin, and other Modernist women writers, "make sense of and reconcile traditional gender roles with recent dismantling of gender construction" (Podnieks 65). Also, the emphasis on writing about sexuality places Nin among the other female Modernist writers who, as noted by Shari Benstock in *Women Writers in Exile*, "discovered sexualized writing identities in expatriation – and in doing so they changed the history of modern women's writing, charting the terrain of female sexuality from female perspectives" (Benstock 28).

For Nin, writing about her sexuality and exploring a nascent literary style alongside Henry Miller in the early 1930s adds a critical context to her own experimentation with language. Nin's eagerness to develop her craft is recorded in *Henry and June*, posthumously published and edited to underscore Nin's creative, lascivious and at times intense relationship with Henry and his wife, June Miller. Nin writes: "I have written thirty pages about June in an intense and wholly imaginative manner, the best I have done so far. It is good to see all the laboratory experiments culminate in a lyrical outburst" (*HJ*:236). She seems pleased with the results of probing her imagination in a "laboratory"-like manner to yield a "lyrical outburst." Nin occasionally relied on Miller's notes describing his relationship with June. She notes: "I read him what I wrote on the effect of his notes. He said I could only write like that, with imaginative intensity because I had not lived out what I was writing about, that the living-out kills the imagination and the intensity, as happens to him" (*HJ*: 54). Using Miller's observations helps Nin create an interpretation of what she "had not lived out," in a relationship with June. This reveals pivotal experiences of ardently working toward developing her craft. However, there were troubling consequences to maturing her art alongside Miller: "As I was working today I realized that I had given away to Henry many of my ideas on June and that he is using them. I feel impoverished, and he knows it, because he writes me that he feels like a crook. What was left for me to do?" (*HJ*: 233). A close reading of Nin's early diaries discloses not only the source of inspiration for her experimental style with frank language and provocative metaphors, but also the sexist context of her time. I will return to discuss the unexpurgated diary *Henry and June* later in this chapter.

Moreover, Nin's patient-therapist relationship with Allendy devolves into a dependence reminiscent of a child on a father. In November 1932, Nin remarks on Allendy as the source of her "newborn strength." She writes: "And tonight I need him . . . He is my father, my god – all in one" (*Incest* 55). At this point, Nin is clearly preoccupied with a perpetual search for a father that is linked with a "god" image. She was aware that her affair with Allendy was propelled by the vivid confusion stemming from the Christian narratives giving rise to a sense of male hubris, as I discuss in Chapter 2, as well as her experiences with sexual abuse, and abandonment, by her father. In fact, the obsession with her father inspires Nin to pursue insights into the psychology of erotic love. Specifically, in a diary entry dated February 16, 1931, Nin records reading Jung's *Psychology and the Unconsciousness*, "attentively and actively" (*ED* 4:386). Nin would have read that according to Jung, that erotic impression between daughters and fathers develops early in a child's life. Jung writes, "among young girls at the time of their first love, remarkable difficulties develop in the capacity for erotic expression, which may be reduced analytically to disturbances through a regressive attempt at resuscitation of the father image," or the "Father-Imago" (*Psychology of the Unconsciousness* 55). Nin used emerging psychological theories, and religious language and imagery, as the basis for her method to transgress the struggle with the relationship between politics, self and religion and her own creativity. Nin played the role of seductress to get what she most wanted: to write an experimental narrative of her own. Like the trickstar, she needed to ask herself the pivotal question: What kind of seductress did she want to be? I will return to this point.

As noted earlier in this chapter, Nin was introduced to Otto Rank's work in the early 1930s by reading Rank's revolutionary book outlining creativity and the artist, in *Art and Artist: Creative Urge and Personality Development* (1932). Nin's initial response to this book was that it is "the book [she] wanted to write!" (*Incest* 73). In this work, Rank considers the ubiquity of the Oedipus complex at the time to suggest that artists themselves "react more strongly than and certainly in a different way from, the normal person to this unavoidable average experience of the paternal relation" (64). The Oedipus complex, according to Rank, was linked to the desire for independence in "human development" (65). His conclusion is that by engaging in the mythical account, the artist can then:

> deliberately make his own by embodying it in action and experience. This experience is a creative experience, for it serves to create the myth itself, and the sagas, poems, and tragedies based on it, whose various representations of the one theme are determined by the collective ideological outlook of the moment and the interpretation appropriate thereof.
>
> (65)

Rank places importance on the ways in which artists symbolically capture their respective experiences with Oedipal energies in myth, as rooted in the zeitgeist.

It is not a coincidence, therefore, that Rank would help Nin transform her diary writing into fiction in the 1930s.

Nin and Rank's analyst-analyzed relationship began in November 1933. This was a seemingly inevitable match, being that Nin at the time considered herself the artist Rank researched and wrote about (1:270). In the *Incest: From a Journal of Love* diary, Nin proclaims her reason for soliciting Rank's guidance: she "felt at the present [she] was expending too much energy trying to master a confusion of desires which [she] could not solve. [She] needed his help" (*Incest*: 291–292). In Nin's description, we understand what Sharon Spencer, in her thoughtful essay "Beyond Therapy: The Enduring Love of Anaïs Nin for Otto Rank," notes were the motives for seeking Rank's guidance: Nin's "difficulty establishing physical and emotional independence of her father, an obsession that came close to crippling her entire life, and an obsession with her frustrated efforts to become an artist" (99). In the ensuing years, Rank would guide Nin through her own creative process following a reunion with her father, Joaquin Nin, in early 1933.

However, Nin understood that Rank "only took cases which interested him" (*Incest* 294). It was therefore important to maintain Rank's curiosity about her as an analysand. One way to do so was to rely on the trickstar spirit through her imagination, including metaphors; for Nin was, after all, seeking guidance to restore stability to what radiated a disintegrating world. In the unexpurgated *Incest* diary, Nin makes known, to her confidante, her diary: "I began to invent what I will tell Rank instead of coordinating truths . . . I prepare myself for a false comedy, like the one I played for Allendy . . . I am going to Rank . . . to aggrandize, dramatize my conflicts" (*Incest* 293). The drama Nin sought to "aggrandize" was focused in her fiction, for on November 8, 1933, Rank dissuaded Nin from compulsively writing in her diary in efforts to focus solely on writing fiction. Nin's response was: "It was a bold stroke. It stunned me. It was a violation" (*Incest* 294). Encouraging Nin to focus on her fiction writing is one of the ways that Sharon Spencer sees that Rank served the role of a "muse" and a "midwife" (Spencer 108). Spencer points out that it was Rank who facilitated "the creative process which brought to light *House of Incest*," as well as *Winter of Artifice* (104). As for Nin's diaries, Rank came to appreciate them for their archetypal qualities, as he saw the diaries containing the symbolic story of a woman's quest toward wholeness in a patriarchal world that could be hostile to women. Nin explains that Rank saw the dairy as a replacement for her father, and that "lesbian tendencies were probably more imaginative than physical" (*Incest* 297–298). These insights liberate Nin and eventually lead to healing. Moreover, in 1934, Nin and Rank become lovers, and later, in 1934, Nin joined him in New York to practice as an apprentice psychotherapist. Sharon Spencer observes that "in addition to the well-known seductive phenomenon of transference and counter-transference – so brilliantly depicted in Nin's portrayal of her period as Rank's assistant, 'The Voice' – there is Nin's already legendary sexual charisma" at play between the two (101).

While Rank was one of Nin's therapist who had the most broad-minded views of feminine creativity at the time, his views on women as artists were nonetheless sexist. Also, the fact that psychologists during Nin's therapy-seeking years did not refrain from patient-client sexual entanglements, to help better empower pioneering women, underscores Nin's ardent desire to create and propel her own literary achievements against masculine ideologies. Nin had the tremendous courage it took to risk exploring the depths of her own psychological reality and those of her characters in order to construct her own mythopoesis. As already noted in this book, Nin's own interest in discovering a language to both know and experience the mystery, trauma and sense of a fragmented self, joins with the field of psychology. Through the passing of time, Nin would consider that the role psychology played was pivotal in the absence of religion: "Psychoanalysis is our only way to gaining wisdom because we no longer have religion" (3:241). She saw psychology as a type of cosmology that included an explanation of mystery and existential meaning. Furthermore, Nin contributed literary works depicting the unfolding creative and psychological process of an astounding woman devoted to artistic creation despite persistent and concurrent, and at times paralyzing, fear that her efforts would be regarded unworthy. We also know that Rank's evolving theories on feminine psychology that he was working on at the time could not have unfolded without his relationship – both intimate and therapist-patient – with Nin.[7]

It is unsurprising, within the context of these evolving psychological concepts, that we find incest as a literary motif in the works of Modernist writers James Joyce, Virginia Woolf, Anaïs Nin and Djuna Barnes.[8] Nin's first use of incest as a metaphor was in *House of Incest* (1931), then again in 1933 as part of the posthumously published *Incest: From a Journal of Love*. Later that year, she wrote *Winter of Artifice*, weaving incest through the novel's plot. The pervasiveness of intellectual interest around sexual awakenings and the mythic roots of Western consciousness at the time elucidates Nin's own preoccupation, treatment and exploration of an incest motif in her unexpurgated diaries, specifically Journal Book 42, posthumously published in *Incest: From a Journal of Love*. By initiating herself into the pivotal metaphor invading not only her psyche, but also that of the cultural milieu, Nin created a language with which to narrate all aspects of self and life experiences, including events happening within the interior subterranean places of psyche and self. Thus, the historical significance of the attention centered around incest fantasy is on one hand inseparable from Nin's own, as captured in the posthumously published *Incest: From a Journal of Love*.

On the other hand, while Nin openly credits the emerging field of psychology as contributing to her sense of self as an artist, psychology alone does not explain the entire power behind Nin's *Incest: From a Journal of Love* narrative. Specifically, it is not my contention that Nin's *Incest: From a Journal of Love* should be reduced to a mere expression of an Oedipal-like trauma. Rather, it is essential that we also see the importance of the *Incest: From a Journal of Love* diaries as a transposition, a reordering of cosmos including a *nykeia* (underworld journey), and ultimately the revival of self through a mythopoesis of her own. This is of literary interest. We should consider Nin's

Incest: From a Journal of Love diaries as embodying characteristics of a Modernist text both thematic and stylistic, depicting the unconscious motivations propelling her erotic life. Hence, Nin reveals the complex relationship between sexuality, fantasy and reality. Also, central to my consideration of Nin's posthumously published diaries *Incest: From a Journal of Love* is the question, in what ways does this collection illuminate Nin's other writings? For example, what does an analysis of the ubiquitous incest theme in Nin's short stories *House of Incest* and *Winter of Artifice* reveal about Nin's creative process when put into dialogue with the concurrent unexpurgated *Early Diaries* and *Incest: From a Journal of Love* diaries, respectively? Could it be possible that what Nin hoped for readers, in the 21st century, was to gain a better understanding of how a woman navigated male ideologies at the time, creating a feminine identity independent of men? This quest, Nin was aware, was not only hers alone. Rather the quest is archetypal. Within the polyphony of voices included in Nin's *Incest: From A Journal of Love* diary, we hear emotions and experiences that are not always those associated with the feminine, including revulsion, aggression, pleasure and death, as well as life. We notice the resonance of an artist through a trickstar spirit, struggling to navigate and prevail over modern patriarchy.

Before turning to Nin's *Incest: From A Journal of Love*, it is important to point out that an incest motif is prevalent in Nin's unexpurgated diaries only, reminding us that there are two types of diaries in Nin's opus: the expurgated and the unexpurgated. The expurgated diaries are *Volumes One* through *Seven*, dated 1931–1974, first published in 1965. Then there are the four volumes of unexpurgated diaries, which were published posthumously and edited by someone else. Two of these unexpurgated diaries were explicitly edited to emphasize a sexual awakening: *Henry and June* (1931–1932) and *Incest: From A Journal of Love* (1932–1933). The remaining two diaries in the unexpurgated collection are *Fire*, revealing Nin's affair with Otto Rank, and *Near the Moon*, which records Nin's affair with Gonzalo. All four of these latter collections were published posthumously starting in the late 1980s. The focus of my analysis will be on *Incest: From A Journal of Love*, published posthumously in 1992, for this is the diary collection that depicts a textual incest and to which I had access to in Nin's original archives.

A costumed incest

Incest: From a Journal of Love opens in October 1932, and revolves around rivalry love affairs with Henry Miller, René Allendy and Antonin Artaud during her marriage to Hugo Guiler. The next year, Nin was reunited with her father and confronts complex and incestuous fantasies. Nin sought equality in the erotic sphere as well as psychic balance, all the while developing her craft as a writer; she created a narrative revealing a woman navigating between the sacred and the profane in a mysterious and sexualized world. As recorded in the opening pages of *Incest: From A Journal of Love*, stemming from diary book titled "La Folle Lucide," Nin sets a mythic stage for a narrative wherein bemused libido propels the juxtaposition of seducer and seeker. In the beginning of this diary, Nin "awaits visitors." She claims these visitors have contributed to a "newborn core" (*Incest* 1). The "gifts" that Nin feels bestowed with relate to a deeper grasp of her desires, and perception of self through sexual engagement. Nin delves into the *nykeia* world made up of obscurities, disenfranchising political power structures, shadows and untamed libido, lurking in the patriarchal context of her time. Nin describes the strain of facing shadows, including untamed sexual desires, as "a great choking pain," a visceral deprivation of oxygen (*Incest* 3). She feels a need to disentangle herself out of "darkness" and knows that the only way to sort out her entanglement is to confront what must be tended. Where better to do this than in her diary, a mode that explicitly invites, and allows, Nin to make narrative sense of experiences through a creative process of her own? Also, like any protagonist navigating the underworld, Nin's rejoinder includes touching upon the sinful, deceitful and the fringes of evil.

One way that Nin saw fit to confront what must be tended was by evoking the seductress, a guise of the costumed self. Nin inverts traditional gender roles by placing herself in the center as seducer with the men as the sex objects. She further designates the role of her diary as a record of her sexual amusement. Nin writes, "This will be the journal of my enjoyment" (*Incest* 153). Nin is the "new kind of enchantress," as she admits to traversing new territory in the guise of a "species of seductress not often encountered" (*Incest* 185). As discussed in the previous Chapter, and as also pointed out by Podnieks, "one of the things Nin most wanted was revenge, and thus she appropriated the role that would empower her to this end: that of the femme fatale" (Podnieks 319). One of the various identities that Nin clung to was that of seducer/seeker; this is validated by her father when he proclaims: "They will take you as my mistress" (*Incest* 160). Nin's experimentation with how far she could push this role is pivotal to her unfolding incest narrative. She writes: "I am interested not in the game, as Don Juan was, *the game of seduction, of maddening, of possessing men not only physically but their souls, too*" (*Incest* 185). The candor as well as heightened emotional language with which Nin writes about fulfilling her role as a seductress reveals a simultaneous sense of repulsion, confusion and delight.

Moreover, in the *Incest: From A Journal of Love* diary entry dated March 9, 1933 Nin writes: "Eduardo, who is so pleased with my dream book, thinks I have found my style, that my erotic, crapulous, decadent writing is the contrary of my Rimbaudian terrific innocence (see how many believe in my innocence – would this journal deceive them?) that I am leaping out, imaginatively, out and beyond my horoscope" (*Incest* 118). The tension between innocence and deception in a poetic style reveals another link between Nin's ardent desire to develop her craft as a writer and create a language of emotional clarity that ultimately reveals dimensions of a woman's invisible geography, including feminine sexuality. In the above passage, Nin credits her newly found "style," which unfolds in *Incest: From a Journal of Love*, with the capacity to "deceive." We hear echoes of Nin's Modernist agenda: to work with the elements of fantasy and reality widespread in the writer's own life, including experiences and curiosities with complex relations between sexes. It is this style that comprises Nin's mythopoesis, bolstering her reordering of her passions.

In a posthumous published diary entry dated May 5, 1933, Nin writes about meeting her father, following a 20-year hiatus: "I have found my father, the God, only to discover that I do not need him. When he comes to me, he who has marked my childhood so deeply, I am already woman, and I am liberated of the need of Father and god" (*Incest* 152). In this passage, Nin repeats an earlier reference to "Father and God" in the description of her subsequent relationship with Allendy. In the latter, she refers to being dependent on Allendy as a source of "newborn strength" and as: "He is my father, my god – all in one" (*Incest* 55). In this passage she references her father echoing the same description of "father, the God." Nin, then, sees herself as "already" a "woman," and he is "again the man who is also child," immature and incapable of providing paternal love (*Incest* 152). By using definitive statements too, such as "I do not need," and "I am so absolutely," Nin suggests a certainty that overrides any ambiguity in her symbolic perception. For Nin comprehends that the separation from her father, and all God-like powers in patriarchy, places her closer to a sense of self as an artist. To rid herself of oppressive structures by first metaphorically fusing with it through an incest metaphor represented in "Father" and "God," suggests the possibility of a new myth from which to create. This newly created myth assures Nin that creativity can occur outside of monotheism.

Later in the same entry, she credits the encounter as bringing her great clarity. Nin writes that it was "not a meeting but a realization of the impossibility of meeting on earth except as man and woman, in the completeness of sex. I lose my terror, my pain, the sacrilegious passion" (*Incest* 152). She reinforces a desire to liberate herself of both the man who terrorized her as a child and the oppressive image of God in the Catholicism of her upbringing. Therefore, freedom from the illusory and elevated image of her father results in freedom from the hold that patriarchal culture through religion has on her gender.

Extricating herself from such terror requires tremendous effort to confront and comprehend her feelings for her father, including scrutiny of his physical appearance. Nin seeks to reconcile his outer appearance of coldness and stiffness with the inner mystery of his being, which she believes he wishes to "conceal." Ultimately, hinting at incest, Nin wishes to integrate these very same parts of her own being. But first, Nin records how frail he is. She writes: "First day of father story. King father arrives after conquering a paralyzing lumbago pale. Suffering. Impatient to come" (*Incest* 204). She observes his demeanor as "cold" and "formal," and his capacity to "conceal" and appear in a "mask." Intrigued, she keeps a laser focus on him, as well as herself. It is this sharp perception of both her own challenges as well as her father's that will translate into her cast of characters in *Winter of Artifice*, which I discuss in Chapter 5.

During this early encounter, Nin saw her father's vulnerability, "pride," "vanity," including "his hatred of showing himself weak, sick, at a disadvantage," and grasps his regard for creating illusions (*Incest* 204). These are the attributes that Nin believes are her own. She writes: "And at the same moment that I saw these traits in Father, I saw them starkly in myself. The coquetry. The fear of intimacy. The inordinate respect of illusion" (*Incest* 204). Witnessing her father "weak" and "sick," means that Nin also experiences him through paradoxical human traits and illusions that she too grapples with. He is a figment of her creation as much as she is his. She comes to perceive him as her "double," which ultimately leads Nin to reject him. What is more, the emphasis on Joaquin Nin's "weak" body as he experiences severe aches and pains throughout the next day when he "could not move from his bed," foreshadows that she will prevail over her own body/narrative. Interestingly, within the drama of incest, it is curious indeed that while Joaquin moves around in an aching body, this is the same day that repeated physical intimacy ensues, as Nin writes: "We kissed, and that kiss unleashed a wave of desire. I was lying across his body and with my breast I felt his desire, hard palpitating . . . more terror than joy. The joy of something un-nameable, obscure. He so beautiful – godlike and womanly, seductive and chiseled, hard and soft. A hard passion" (*Incest* 209). This description, once again, echoes Nin's depiction of the painting *Lot and His Daughters* in *House of Incest*. I considered this passage earlier in this chapter, but it bears repeating here. In the painting, Lot embraces his daughter with one hand "upon his daughter's breast," which she flaunts, and they experience the "joy and terror of their love." This experience in the novella is depicted as a moment that brings the daughter a sense of the power she clinches over her father. In this *Incest: From a Journal of Love* diary, the sexualized experience between Nin and her father is captured through the emphasis on breasts, conveying the erotic and sexualized daughter, and corresponding emotions involving "joy" as well as "terror," also reflected in the painting *Lot and His Daughters*. In her own description, Nin draws close parallels between her incest narrative and the mythic story captured in the painting *Lot and His Daughters*. The imagery in this biblical reference serves Nin's own narrative, as it juxtaposes incest as part of Judeo-Christian history.

In a later diary entry, Nin pursues the theme of evil and revenge. She writes: "I feel supremely innocent, yet I have done evil. I have committed all the sacrileges . . . I am wreaking a kind of revenge upon men" (*Incest* 196). To expound on these themes, I turn to Elizabeth Podnieks's comprehensive analysis of this topic. Central to Podnieks's study of Nin's posthumously published *Incest: From a Journal of Love* is the notion that Nin "made her diary the whistle she blew against [her father]. She has had the last word, and it is one of 'ruthless truth' indeed, her final and unequivocal 'revenge upon men'" (332). Podnieks underscores that while Nin does yield to the power her father holds on her because of her desire for paternal love, "there was clearly a part of her which was able to stand back, record her repulsion, and recognize the abuse that had gone on" (332). Evidence of this is found in a diary entry dated June 10, 1934 wherein Nin writes of her father: "And I smile to see I have no emotion – no feeling for this stiff inhuman schoolteacher" (*Incest* 339). I will return to these points shortly.

The following months gave way to an exchange of correspondence between Nin and her father. A close look at the prose of these letters is worth noting, as they reveal intimately related descriptions, themes and emotions.[9] In a letter to her father Nin writes:

> Our lives have been full of effort, herculean struggles to climb, to surpass ourselves in everything, to make great souls of ourselves, to perfect, to develop, to evolve – almost painfully difficult ascensions, aiming ever higher, always in pursuit of new visions, rejecting what we were yesterday.
>
> (*Incest* 246)

Nin's letter has a reflective tone as she ponders the "herculean struggles" she has endured. Words such as "great," "perfect," "evolve," "ascensions" and "pursuit" reflect determination in a heroic life. When reading her father's response, one cannot help but notice the reverberating theme and pensive tone. He responds in kind:

> I won't even try to reply to this morning's beautiful letter. I doubt very much that I possess all the treasures with which your love endows me. But if I am not as you see me, it is certain that all my life I have wanted to be something very similar, an approximation of it. If throughout my life, by a superhuman and continuous effort, without fear or flinching, struggling against everything and everyone, I modeled my soul, chiseled my spirit, sublimated my heart, and harmonized all the trembling of my being, this was the obscure target I aimed at, hardly daring to admit it even to myself.
>
> (*Incest* 248)

The above letter shares the introspective tone of Nin's letter, as they both ponder the "superhuman" strength required to get what they respectively need out of life. This letter also uses words referring to focus and resolve in averting "struggle:" "harmonized," "target" and "aimed." Also, one cannot help but notice that the word "chiseled" was used in Nin's own description of her father's appearance in their early encounter, as previously noted ("He is so beautiful – godlike and womanly, seductive and chiseled, hard and soft. A hard passion" [209]). Both letters make use of comparable emotional language: Nin references life in totality by stating, "our lives have been full of effort" (*Incest* 246). Her father's letter also makes reference to the entirety of his life: he writes, "it is certain that all my life I have wanted something" (*Incest* 248). The parallels in the elevated and emotional writing, and the comparable states of mind and feelings mirrored in each letter, indicate Nin's consideration that she and her father are symbolic representations of one another.

The distinct paralleling and re-claiming of experiences in Nin's prose throughout *Incest: From a Journal of Love* is also discussed by Podnieks in her analysis of Nin's piquant moments, first with Artaud and later with her father. Podnieks points to "Nin's performances with Artaud" as "prefigur[ing] incestuous directions that her relationship with her father would take" (325). Podnieks analyzes Nin's descriptions of her experiences with her father thus:

> His advances were threatening; though her body responded to his touch, 'all the while some part of me was hard and terrified.' Nonetheless, 'with a strange violence, I lifted my negligee and I lay over him.' Though he 'emptied all of himself in me,' Nin was unable to have an orgasm because of the 'core of fear' that prevented it. After sex, she admitted that she felt 'revulsion [. . .] I wanted to run away'. She felt 'poisoned by this union,' and she repeated 'poison' three times."
>
> (*Podnieks* 326)

By carefully isolating this passage, Podnieks concludes that Nin "figures as both the performer and the spectator, an appropriate role for the participant in the Theatre of Cruelty" (326). Also, Nin's depiction of her affair with Artaud has parallels to the description of an encounter with her father. Podnieks notes that " 'to be kissed by Artaud was to be poisoned' is matched by [Nin's] feelings of being 'poisoned' by her father" (326). Consequently, Podnieks links the "drama of incest" with Nin's "interpretation" of Artaud's Theater of Cruelty, which Nin was keenly aware of at the time (Podnieks 322–323). Also, Nin shared Artaud's preoccupation with incest as a metaphor, seen in their mutual fascination with Lucas van Leyden's painting *Lot and His Daughters*.

In Nin's diary, *Volume One*, in an entry dated June, 1933, Nin copies a letter sent to her by Artaud wherein he captures her memorable reaction to the painting *Lot and His Daughters*:

> I have brought many people, men and women, to see the marvelous painting [*Lot and His Daughters*] but it is the first time I have seen an artistic reaction move a being and make vibrate like love. Your senses trembled, and I realized that, in you, the body and the spirit are completely welded, if a pure spiritual impression can stir up such a storm in you.
>
> (1:232)

Nin was indeed deeply inspired by this painting, and it was with "artistic" interest that she would capture her own portrayal of incest. So while Lucas van Leyden used bold and colorful strokes to capture erotic and incestuous impulses, Nin did the same with forward and audacious language. Also, Artaud's reference to Nin being "stir[red]" at the core speaks to the references Nin makes to her father about the painting that year. In her *Incest: From a Journal of Love* Nin notes: "I told him about the painting of Lot and his daughters. He said, 'You are still a child.' But I remembered he had said the first night '*Je n'ai plus de Dieu*! – I have lost God'" (*Incest* 212).

Moreover, the sexual encounter between Nin and her father is described as enacted through "superhuman" strength: "The next night, when he was a little freer in his movements and he lay over me, it was an orgy, and he penetrated me three and four times without pausing and without withdrawing – his new strength, new desire, and new spurt coming like waves following each other . . . I plunged into the completion of his" (*Incest* 212). Furthermore, Podnieks adds that "to be sure, Artaud's 'unleashing' is precisely the word that Nin used to describe the impact of her father: 'that kiss unleashed a wave of desire'" (Podnieks 327). Podnieks rightly sees Nin's greatest desire to be that of "control[ing] her body/text" (Podnieks 327). I contend that it is in the realm of the female trickster that Nin can both "unleash" and initiate incestuous gestures, through her own symbolic and literary style, to create her own incest narrative. This incest narrative could after all be the expression of the "creative experience" that Rank proposed would "serve to create the myth itself," which Nin develops in *Winter of Artifice* (Rank 65).

While I agree with the accuracy of Podnieks's evaluation, I would also argue that Nin's *Incest: From a Journal of Love* was written in efforts to liberate herself from unexamined passions and fantasies. Nin initially turns to writing to help orchestrate her experiences, especially those of a threatening world, including oppression and abuse toward women. As a child, Nin was the victim of sexual abuse by her father, who later abandoned the entire family (Podnieks 299). When reflecting on her childhood experiences, Nin writes: "My father did not want a girl. My father was over-critical. He was never satisfied, never pleased. I never remember a compliment or a caress from him. At home, only scenes, quarrels, beatings. And his hard blue eyes on us, looking for the flaws" (1:76). Nin often saw her father's actions towards women as representative of patriarchal violence. Throughout her life, Nin made a connection between the patterns of emotional dependency on an absent father, oppressive cultural and religious constructs, and a sense of blocked libido. In an interview in 1972, Nin stated:

> Then there is another thing which plagues women, which comes also from the culture, it comes from religion, it comes from the family . . . Our culture tells the man that he has to go beyond the personal because he has to achieve. He is excused for not being a particularly good father, or a particularly good son, or whatever it is that he doesn't fulfill in the personal life.
>
> (*A Woman Speaks* 40–41)

By being keenly aware of the cultural paradigms of her time, Nin emphasized that through the dedication to her craft where "every spiritual thought was made visible," she could offer the world a reinvigorated portrait of humanity. Nin writes: "Yet woman gains something from this great emphasis on the personal life . . . a very great humanism" (*A Woman Speaks* 41). These were psychological complexities into which Nin sought insight, often distraughtly, in the works of Freud, Jung and Rank in the 1920s and 1930s, as recorded in her unexpurgated diaries. Nin created a narrative that textually explores not only the feminine qualities by which she felt entrapped and plagued, but also contains harsh observations of masculine traits, as she reveals the lamentable behavior of the men in her life at the time.

Nin needed desperately to restore faith in her sense of self as an artist. She had a penchant for writing metaphorically; through a trickster temperament, she initiates a language to create an incest narrative of her own. What is more, *Incest: From a Journal of Love* could parallel the symbolic incest derivative of androcentric ideologies incapable of granting women their autonomy as artists and creators of their own narratives. Perhaps it was only by creating her own incest narrative that Nin could metaphorically mirror back, from a female subject position, the destructive effects of misguided sexual desires being projected onto women at the time.

After the storm: navigating the world of the posthumously published unexpurgated diaries

Given the sensationalizing and polemic that ensued with the posthumous publication of *Incest: From a Journal of Love*, in 1992, we could ask: what would Nin have believed her literary reputation had to gain by publishing her unexpurgated diaries six decades after they were written? The introduction states that "now that virtually all of the people referred to in *Incest: From A Journal of Love* have died, there is no cause to hold back on publishing the diary as Anaïs wished: in unexpurgated form" (ix). It is also stated that following the publication of these unexpurgated works, the world will have "an extraordinary lifetime record of the emotional growth of a creative artist" (*Incest* x). This collection, we are told in the preface, is composed of Diary Books 37 through 46, dated 1932–1934. The note at the end of the preface informs us:

> The text of *Incest* is taken from diary books thirty-seven through forty-six, as numbered by Anaïs Nin. Her titles for these ten books were "*La Folle Lucide*," "*Equilibre*," "Uranus," "*Schizoidie and Paranoia*," "The Triumph of Magic – White and Black Magic," "Flagellation," "And on the Seventh Day He Rested from his Work, Quoted Negligently from a Book I Never Read," "*Audace*," "The Definite Appearance of the Demon," and "Flow – Childhood – Rebirth."
>
> (*Incest* xi)

It is true in looking through the original diary books at the UCLA archives that I found that Nin assigned its own title to each individual Diary Book (with the exception of Diary Book 43).[10] However, while there are indeed ten books listed above, a careful review of these titles in the archival material reveal that the list above accounts for only eight of the ten Diary Books 37 through 46; the titles for two of these diary books are listed as four separate titles, when they are actually only two. Table 4.1 lists journals 37 through 46 as they appear in the archives, as Nin actually titled them:

Table 4.1 Original Titles for Journal Books 37 through 46

Journal Number	*Title*
37	La Folle Lucide/Equilibre
38	Uranus
39	Schizoidie and Paranoia/The Triumph of Magic – Black and White Magic!
40	Flagellation
41	"And on the Seventh Day He Rested from His Work," Quoted Negligently from a Book I Never Read
42	Incest
43	(No title)
44	Audace
45	The Definite Appearance of the Demon
46	Flow – Child – Birth – Rebirth

The above shows that Nin incorporates two titles in Diary Books 37 and 39, yet they are listed as separate titles in the Preface. Diary Book 37 is entitled as follows (presented on the page on two separate lines):

> *La Folle Lucide*
> *Equilibre*

The same is true for Diary Book 39, which also Nin titled on two separate lines:

> Schizoidie and Paranoia,
> The Triumph of Magic – White and Black Magic!

It is also curious that while the same introduction indicates that this publication contains Diary Books 37 through 46, Diary number 42, the one Diary Book Nin herself titles "Incest," in which she recounts in great detail an affair with her father in the months of June 1933–August 1933, is nonetheless omitted from the list of diaries in the preface. Yet much later in *Incest: From a Journal of Love*, the reader is treated with a photograph of the title page of Diary Book 42, slipped in-between the published diary pages detailing Nin's racy interaction with her father on June 23, 1933. I was fortunate to have access to the original material, but without this exposure, one would not understand that Nin had but one single Diary Book that she herself titled "Incest." Why then, the omission of this seemingly important title from the list of journals comprising the book, only to have it surface 211 pages later, at the height of perhaps the most scandalous and titillating scene of the unexpurgated diaries? In the posthumously published *Incest: From A Journal of Love*, Diary Book 42 comprises three months of the book's two-year span, or only 49 of the 403 pages. It seems that featuring the word "incest" in the title lends itself indeed to the misconception that diary books 37 through 46 are entirely about father/daughter incestuous love.

Likewise, the editing of Nin's unexpurgated diaries dating from 1931 to 1932 posthumously published in 1986 under the title *Henry and June*, contains a similar rearrangement of Nin's original organization and edited content. However, in *Henry and June* we gain insight into the editorial motivation for doing so. In the preface, we learn that "[t]he present volume reexamines that period from a new perspective, releasing material deleted from the original diary and never before published. It was Anaïs's wish to have the full story told" (*HJ*: ix). Then, the paragraph that follows explains what is meant by "full story." It reads: "The text is taken from journals thirty-two through thirty-six, titled 'June,' 'The Possessed,' 'Henry,' 'Apotheosis and Downfall,' and 'Journal of the Possessed,' written from October 1931 to October 1932. It has been edited to focus on the story of Anaïs, Henry, and June" (*HJ*: IX). Here it is indicated that rather than this version containing the "full story" it has actually been "edited to focus on the story of Anaïs, Henry, and June." One could ask: if it is indeed the full story that these editors were hoping to capture according to Nin's wish, why not publish the diaries as they are, as Nin left them? Why interfere in editing and shaping the material in Nin's absence? And again, the diary books that are listed above, as noted in the preface, do not coincide with the titles of the originals located in the UCLA archives. For example, Diary Book 33 is titled: "June, Henry, Eduardo." In the preface, this single title appears as two separate titles, "June" and "Henry," and the actual title of Diary Book 33 is omitted. (Nin's Diary Book 32 is titled "June.") Also, Diary Book number 35 is titled "Henry The Apotheosis and Downfall." In the list of diaries in the preface, the latter is presented as two separate titles ("'Henry' and 'Apotheosis and Downfall'" [*HJ* ix]), once more distorting how Nin herself organized her content. Moreover, *Henry and June* is edited to shape a particular story about Nin's life, and we must remember that equally important as what appears on the pages is what is omitted. While this posthumous publication aims at celebrating, we are told, Nin's "experiments in erotic writing," the content does not appear in the way that Nin herself organized her prose. Rather, the content is organized and edited in a way that underscores a particular story construed by the editors of Nin's collection, not Nin herself. Therefore, when reading *Incest: From A Journal of Love*, we could assume that, like *Henry and June*, it is edited to place emphasis on the relationship between Nin and her father, one that details an incestuous encounter.

Also, one wonders why the editors of these diaries would break from Nin's own nomenclature of titling the diaries by volume number, as in other of her unexpurgated volumes.[11] What was the intention in titling this unexpurgated, posthumously published edition, *Incest: From A Journal of Love*, editing the content to underscore experiences taken from one diary book, then omitting it from the list of content contained in the publication? Publishing these diaries under the title *Incest: From A Journal of Love*, the editors reduce the entire collection to Nin's alleged incest. We must question whether Nin could have anticipated the sensationalizing that ensued after the publishing of *Incest: From a Journal of Love* in 1992 that tends to dominate her literary reputation even today.[12] It seems that while Nin sought recognition for a pioneering literary style and lifestyle during the 1920s and 1930s, in her later years, the mature Nin, the inspired and courageous artist creating a mode of her own, was eager to leave a literary legacy to be read and studied, not mired in scandal. She would not have intended to be reduced to a limited, highly traumatic and experimental time in her life, which evokes the trickstar initiator and creator spirit both in its provocative and ambiguous disguise.

When conjecturing on how Nin would have responded to the queries raised here, I rely on statements she made in interviews in the late 1960s to early 1970s. In the winter of 1969, Daisy Aldan asked Nin how she determined what to edit out of the diary. Aldan reported to Nin that some of her readers were disappointed the diaries do not reveal "intimacies and scandal" (*A Woman Speaks* 177). Nin's poignant response was that "certain intimate aspects of one's life and that of others should be preserved. Scandal obscures rather than enhances the deeper meaning of experience" (177). The latter suggests that Nin would have somewhat suspected the publishing of her unexpurgated diaries, detailing a taboo subject, would result in sensationalizing. Nin's lifelong belief about the essence of art was that it is a portal for revealing the depths of our human experiences, without the need for disgracing the author through gossip-style critique that would then loom over the literary achievements and an extraordinary life. It was after all her contention that the mystery of the "transplantation" of "strong emotion" made its way into literature because of the "strong roots in the base of our emotional nature" (*The Novel of the Future* 57). Three years later, in a letter to a reader in the winter of 1972, Nin reassures the recipient that she was fully aware that the expurgated diaries exclude references to her husband, and the reason for such omission is out of respect for his wish to be excluded. She concludes the letter by reassuring that "someday the entire Diary will be published" (7:252). Here it seems that it was important for Nin to appease the curiosity of her reader by pointing to an obvious reason for the omission of her husband, as well as to the poetic and polyvocal capacity of the diary as a literary genre: its malleable qualities that resemble and assume the shape of its vessel (Kadar 11).

Revelatory remarks are also made about Nin's attitude toward unexpurgated material in the foreword by Gunther Stuhlmann, of *Waste of Timelessness and other Early Short Stories*, where Nin acknowledges: "I had never intended these stories to be published," being that she believed they were "immature." However, she recognized there would be value for a thoughtful and ardent audience that would appreciate her craft. She further writes: "But then I realized that it is valuable for other writers to follow the development of the total work, to observe each step in the maturing process. . . . I was persuaded that these stories would be for those who understand and love my work and are interested in the progression. This is a book for friends only" (2). I propose we likewise consider Nin's posthumously published *Incest: From A Journal of Love* under these gracious circumstances; that is, to acknowledge the *prima materia* of an artist, and as a part of a greater narrative, within an expansive historical, literary and cultural context, which contain complexities in the final editing process. Nin's *Incest: From a Journal of Love* diaries reveal a poetic transposition of cosmos, including a *nykeia* (underworld journey) and ultimately the renewal of self through a mythopoesis of her own.

A discussion of posthumously published material would not be complete without reflecting on the fact that Nin is not the only writer whose husband has overseen the posthumous publication and taken editing license in the process. Leonard Woolf oversaw the editing and publishing of various diaries of Virginia Woolf, also rearranging content and controlling her posthumous reputation.[13] Ted Hughes published Sylvia Plath's *Ariel*, omitting and rearranging content, resulting in a "crafted" depiction of Plath's work.[14] I therefore submit that the posthumous materials should not tether an entire literary oeuvre to "scandal." Rather, when reading unexpurgated posthumous publications, one must see the work as it stands, in its unexpurgated guise, and when polemic ensures, take into account the context in which the work was created, as well as the "husbanding" involved in the conditions under which publication was overseen.[15]

It is also important to underscore that while the incest account may be based on facts, aside from Nin's own account within the incest narrative, there is no actual evidence that she engaged in literal incest with her ill father during the summer of 1933. While the Diary Books comprising *Incest: From A Journal of Love* contain Nin's perpetual efforts to untangle a costumed self, including an assortment of complex feelings about her own sexuality and a lifelong tumultuous relationship with her father, any conclusive historical evidence pointing to literal incest – if it was ever available – is by now long gone. Also, while the letters that Nin and her father exchanged during the time of their reunion reveal deep emotional and poetic ties, they do not explicitly confirm a literal incestuous relationship.

Conclusion: intimacy with the faces of (un)veiled reality

Ultimately, the posthumously published *Incest: From A Journal of Love* does not have to be the last and final word overshadowing Nin's literary achievements. After all, it is important to note, the darkness that unfolds in *Incest: From A Journal of Love* did not result in the slaughter of her family, like in the legendary Oedipus myth, or paralyze Nin for the rest of her life. That is, like any strong denouement, once the narrative reaches a climax, Nin expounds on feeling liberated from her father and rejoices: "Oh, I'm free! I'M FREE!" (*Incest* 339–340).

Although Nin does not untangle all her fantasies nor effectively reorder her sense of self, she is a survivor; an exploration of complex father and daughter relationships continue to unfold in her later fictional works. From the female trickstar's perspective, by the end of *Incest: From A Journal of Love*, Nin restores, to the extent possible, a sense of understanding to her world. She uses her diaries to create a narrative wherein she becomes intimate with the many faces of her reality at the time. Nin harnesses fantasies during a time of emotional turmoil, and through a sense of feminine embodiment, maneuvering the tints and tones of its content, creates a narrative that aids in the burgeoning of the female artist. This means that Nin symbolically emerges on the other side, as we witness in the creation of a refined literary version using incest as a metaphor in *Winter of Artifice*. I will expound on this novel in the next chapter.

Notes

1 The other person Nin is referring to is John Erskine.
2 See a reference to the nascent book that would become *D. H. Lawrence: An Unprofessional Study* in *Early Diary IV*, p. 291.
3 Peter L. Rudnytsky includes a comprehensive cultural and historical context of the emerging field of psychology. This could be found in "Introductory Essay," in Otto Rank's *The Incest Theme in Literature and Legend: Fundamentals of a Psychology of Literary Creation*. London: Johns Hopkins University Press, 1992,
4 In her essay, "Incest in Jung's Work: The Origins of the Epistomophilic Instinct," Coline Covington expounds on the distinctions between Jung's and Freud's incest theories, as well as considers Jung's difficulties in refraining from incestuous quandaries with his patients. This essay is in *Journal of Analytical Psychology*, 2003, 48, 255–262.
5 See Sharon Spencer's essay "Beyond Therapy: The Enduring Love of Anaïs Nin for Otto Rank."
6 Nin reflects on reading Rank's work in *Incest*, p. 73.
7 See Sharon Spencer's "Beyond Therapy: The Enduring Love of Anaïs Nin for Otto Rank" wherein she expounds on Rank's posthumously published book "Feminine Psychology and Masculine Ideology," p. 103.
8 See Bonnie Kime Scott's book *Post Modern Feminist Readings of Woolf, West, and Barnes*. Indianapolis: Indiana University Press. 1995.
9 In Nin's original diary, these letters appear in French in her own handwriting. It was her custom to transcribe her letters onto the diary.
10 I was given permission by The Anaïs Nin Trust to use her original diary titles from the UCLA Archives.
11 Nin titles her diaries *Volumes One–Seven*. (*Volume One*: 1931–1934; *Volume Two*: 1934–1939; *Volume Three*: 1939–1944; *Volume Four*: 1944–1947: *Volume Five*: 1947–1955: *Volume Six*: 1955–1966 and *Volume Seven*: 1966–1974).
12 A basic internet search of Nin's name results in a heightened attention to father and daughter incest as recorded in *Incest: From a Journal of Love*. Critics and readers either admire her highly poetic prose, mythic style and courageous spirit, or despise her as amoral, a liar and mere narcissist.
13 In her book *Virginia Woolf*, Hermione Lee discusses Leonard's role in Woolf's posthumous publications.
14 See *The Restored Edition: Ariel*, published in 2005. The preface of this edition provides insight into the background of the 1965 posthumous publication by Ted Hughes.
15 Hermione Lee's term to describe Leonard's involvement in Virginia Woolf's posthumously published works.

Works cited

Benstock, Shari. *Women of the Left Bank: Paris, 1900–1940*. Texas: Texas UP. 1986. Print.
———. *Women Writers in Exile*. Chapel Hill: The U of North Carolina P. 1989. Print.

Blume, Lesley M. *Everybody Behaves Badly: The True Story Behind Hemingway's Masterpiece The Sun Also Rises*. New York: Houghton Mifflin Harcourt Publishing. 2016. Print.

Hinz, Evelyn J. Ed. *A Woman Speaks: The Lectures, Seminars, and Interviews of Anaïs Nin*. Chicago: Swallow Press. 1975. Print.

Jung, C. G. "Analytical Psychology and Education." *The Development of Personality*, The Collected Works of C. G. Jung. CW Vol. 17, pp. 63–132. Eds. Sir Herbert Reed, Dr. Michael Fordham and Dr. Gerhard Adler, translated by R. F. C. Hull. London: Routledge; Princeton: Princeton UP. (1946–54).

———. "Psychic Conflicts in a Child." *The Development of Personality*. The Collected Works of C. G. Jung. CW Vol. 17, pp. 1–135. Eds. Sir Herbert Reed, Dr. Michael Fordham and Dr. Gerhard Adler, translated by R. F. C. Hull. London: Routledge; Princeton: Princeton UP. (1946–54).

———. "On Psychology of the Unconsciousness." *Two Essays in Analytical Psychology*. The Collected Works of C. G. Jung. CW Vol. 7, pp. 1–119. Eds. Sir Herbert Reed, Dr. Michael Fordham and Dr. Gerhard Adler, translated by R. F. C. Hull. London: Routledge; Princeton: Princeton UP. (1943–66).

———. *Memories, Dreams, Reflections*. New York: Random House. 1989. Print.

Loy, Mina. "Feminist Manifesto." *The Lost Lunar Baedeker: Poems of Mina Loy*. Ed. Roger L. Conover. New York: Farrar, Straus and Giroux. 1996. Print.

Nin, Anaïs. *House of Incest*. Chicago: Swallow Press. 1958. Print.

———. *D. H. Lawrence: An Unprofessional Study*. Chicago: Swallow Press. 1964. Print.

———. *The Diary of Anaïs Nin Volume One (1931–1934)*. New York: Harvest. 1969a. Print.

———. *The Diary of Anaïs Nin Volume Three (1939–1944)*. New York: Harvest. 1969b. Print.

———. *Waste of Timelessness and Other Early Short Stories*. Chicago: Swallow Press. 1977. Print.

———. *The Early Diary of Anaïs Nin, Volume Four (1927–1931)*. New York: Harcourt Brace Jovanovich. 1985. Print.

———. *Henry and June*. New York: Harvest. 1986.

———. *Incest: From A Journal of Love (1932–1934)*. New York: Harcourt Brace Jovanovich. 1992. Print.

———. *Winter of Artifice*. Chicago: Swallow Press. 1945. Print.

Podnieks, Elizabeth. *Daily Modernism: The Literary Diaries of Virginia Woolf, Antonia White, Elizabeth Smart, and Anaïs Nin*. London: McGill-Queen's UP. 2000. Print.

Rank, Otto. *Art and Artist: Creative Urge and Personality Development*. New York: W.W. Norton. 1932. Print.

Rowland, Susan. *The Ecocritical Psyche: Literature, Evolutionary Complexity and Jung*. New York: Routledge. 2012. Print.

Rudnytsky, Peter. "Introduction." *The Incest Theme in Literature and Legend*. Ed. Otto Rank. Baltimore: John Hopkins UP. 1991. Print.

Spencer, Sharon. "Beyond Therapy: The Enduring Love of Anaïs Nin for Otto Rank." *Anaïs Nin: Literary Perspectives*. Ed. Suzanne Nalbantian. New York: St. Martin's Press. 1997. Print.

Chapter 5

The literary credo of a diarist and novelist as traced in *Incest: From A Journal of Love* and *Winter of Artifice*

> We live entirely, especially if we are writers, by the imposition of a narrative line upon disparate images, by the "ideas" with which we have learned to freeze the shifting phantasmagoria which is our actual experience.
>
> (Joan Didion *1978*)

In this chapter I propose that reading *Winter of Artifice* in dialogue with the unexpurgated *Incest: From a Journal of Love* shows the mythopoetic process that links mimesis and ontology of a self. I, and other critics, have already pointed out that Nin's aesthetic attitude toward life meant that what she explored in her diaries, including fantasies, was often transfigured through a creative process into her fiction. To explore this topic, I investigate the intersection of Nin's diarist and novelist credos. It is therefore important to once again reflect on what Nin held to be true about the two distinct human needs connecting life and art: "One is a human need to be intimate with experience," and "[t]hen there's a second need in human nature which is to create something that has more permanence, which is the myth of our lives, the symbolic, spiritual significance of our lives" (*A Woman Speaks* 190). This suggests that an intimate exploration of life in creative terms was wedded to her art. It was the convergence of life and art that remained a perpetual interest throughout Nin's life.

Nin's credo echoes Otto Rank's theory about art and the artist, as explored in Chapter 4. That is, Rank believed that the creative process of the artist includes "deliberately" making "his own embodying in action and experience."[1] According to both Rank, and Nin, creative experience stemming from the personal gave room to construct "the myth itself," which was captured in literature (Rank 65). It was in her diaries that Nin documented experiences including fantasies and psychological realities. I have already argued that the diary, inextricably linked to a space to "relive" her "life in terms of a dream, a myth an endless story," is intimately entwined with personal myth (1:89). In this chapter I argue that in Nin's fiction, the themes already contended with in her diaries are given a multiplicity and mythic dimension (1:89). Nin believed that the interconnection between life and artistic form allowed both diary and fiction a firm place in the world.

Nin writes, "the fiction can reveal the myth behind experience and we need both. We need the myth, the poem, and then we also need this human document from which we get our contact with the self and with our inner life" (*A Woman Speaks* 191). Nin reminds us that the record of the "inner life" contained in her diary was brought into consciousness as part of the material of an individual, revealing the development of the "inner life" of an artist. The unfolding creative process documented throughout 60 years in Nin's diaries affords a window into an archetypal quest of an artist finding a voice, deep within the "seed" of embodiment, amidst a cultural and historical specificity. Moreover, in the fiction, archetypes persist to hold a recognizable world together.

Suzanne Nalbantian's book *Aesthetic Autobiography: From Life to Art in Marcel Proust, James Joyce, Virginia Woolf and Anaïs Nin*, analyzes the role that autobiographical content plays in Modernist fiction. She writes:

> As in the standard autobiographies, "that great Cathedral space which was childhood," as Woolf calls it in "A Sketch of the Past," or the traumatic passageways of adolescence, are featured in these novels. But beyond the standard biographies, these perspectives become the source for the fictionalizing process. For Proust and Woolf, childhood contains elements of an idyllic experience . . . Such a view is recast in some of their fiction, as the perspective of the child marks both *Combray* and *To the Lighthouse*. On the other hand, in the case of Joyce, childhood is marked by repression by his society and his elders – expressed by the author as a "grave of childhood" in *A Portrait*. So too, in Nin, anxiety is attached to the early period of her life, as expressed overtly in her childhood diary *Linotte*.
>
> (51–52)

Essential to the use of autobiographical content in fiction for Proust, Joyce, Woolf and Nin, as posited by Nalbantian, is that "instead of narrating, as does autobiography proper, isolated including as single 'crisis experiences' or turning points with psychological implications, these authors create from the representative scenes" (52).

The "representative scenes," or "symbol making" for Nin, involved transfiguring the personal experiences, including both psychological realism and fantasy, into fiction. Also, believing that the basic intentions of both the diary and fiction were "intimacy with people, with experience, with life itself," Nin not only strove for literary styles that integrated life experiences through a mythic consciousness, but pushed the envelope by taking great risks in exploring taboo subjects (*The Novel of the Future* 155). Unlike other writers, Nin was not interested in obscuring the link between the role of the personal in the fictional as a part of her own creative process. For Nin, personal myth was part of an exploration of collective experiences. Nalbantian recognizes that "while Woolf had declared that the relationship between life and art was very intricate and had sought exterior formal structure and abstraction in her treatment of life materials, Nin went on to deny and blur any separation between her life and her craft" (172). As Nin writes: "There is no separation between my life and my craft, my work. The form of art is the form of my life, and my life is the form of the art" (4:142).

I turn to *Winter of Artifice*, specifically, to consider the discerning craft of the artist as she sorts, orders and polishes the flow of emerging images, illusions, impressions and sensations that are first recorded in the posthumously published *Incest: From a Journal of Love*. On June 23, 1933 Nin writes: "FIRST DAY OF FATHER STORY. King father arrives after conquering a paralyzing lumbago. Pale. Suffering. Impatient to come" (*Incest* 204). The "FIRST DAY" refers to an encounter with her father, as the beginning of a cycle. Earlier that year, on May 5, 1933, Nin writes: "I HAVE FOUND MY FATHER, THE GOD, ONLY TO DISCOVER that I do not need him. When he comes to me, he who has marked my childhood so deeply, I am already woman, and I am liberated of the need of Father and god" (*Incest* 152). The linking of father and god throughout the *Incest* diary, as noted in the previous chapter, reminds us of Nin's propensity to associate wounds inflicted by biological father, lover in Allendy, and father-god all together. All three figures represent forms of patriarchal judgements, as well as edifices of feminine constructs. The fusing of this metaphor, of the split between death and love as ending a cycle, culminates in *Winter of Artifice* in the image of the mystical bride, which I turn to shortly.

On August 8, 1933, Nin reflects: "I have come to the end of a cycle. My life, which began with my passion for Father, ends with the same passion. And *ends*. The cycle of living has come to a close. Now I enter upon peace and work (just like Henry)" (*Incest* 238). When understanding this diary entry within the context of the climax of her "FATHER STORY," (a reference noted on June 23, 1933) one cannot help but see the reference to having reached "an end of a cycle," as pointing to the archetypal cycle of death and rebirth. This means that death of a part of her occurs in order to create art out of fantasy, spiritual and emotional experiences. It is important to note that the diary entry referring to the end of a cycle, dated August 8, 1933, referenced above, marks the final entry in the original Diary Book 42, which Nin calls "Incest."[2] What is more, Nin's reference in this diary entry to her "return" points to a visit from her father that, "something is artistically closed – at least my life's theme, my life's novel. The rest is rounding and polishing and enameling" (*Incest* 238). The sense of closure recorded here comes at a time when Nin's personal encounters with her father are reaching a conclusion. Yet, in fiction, she delves into father and daughter relationships with a keen intensity. This means that the "rounding and polishing and enameling" of the theme of the circular nature of a plurality of experiences in one's life is depicted in *Winter of Artifice*, as well as in later fiction. We are reminded that art was Nin's process which could unfetter her from the labyrinth of selfhood. The liberation unfolded through a mythopoesis of her own. In *Winter of Artifice*, we hear the narrator assert that "[w]hat remained was the slavery to a pattern" (117). Later in the novel it is noted that the protagonist and her father "had been slaves of a pattern, and not of love" (118). The theme is also explored in *Seduction of the Minotaur*, as once Lillian is "journeying homeward" we learn that she moves forward rather than remaining mired in the past: "The detours of the labyrinth did not expose disillusion, but unexplored dimension . . . labyrinths beneath her feet like the excavated passages under Mexico City, but she had feared entering it and meeting the Minotaur" (*Seduction of the Minotaur* 111). The images of labyrinths and monsters links Lillian's experience of a *nykeia* journey to the classic Greek myth involving the Minotaur. (This is the subject of Chapter 6.) Moreover, as is evident in the various textual representations of father-daughter relationships in fiction throughout Nin's life, her creative process was mimetic of "rounding and polishing and enameling" of the emotional relationships as first explored in her diaries. Nin's creative process of drawing from her diaries to write her fiction is unsurprising, as she once noted: "each character had been taken first from a living heart. Whether or not the transplant was successful, I leave to the critics" (*Novel of the Future* 145). She believed in the possibility of the imagination as a "constant deformer," yet as a way to create and construct a compelling sense of selfhood (*D. H. Lawrence* 32).[3]

Nin began writing *Winter of Artifice* in 1933, and completed it in 1934 (1:314). It was published in 1939, the week before World War II began. The use of stream of consciousness allows readers to experience the inner narratives that run deep in the narrator's life. As Djuna operates in a fictional and at times surreal space, readers feel the familiarity of the first-person world of the diary. Djuna's conflicts with dualism unfold in timeless and mythic scenes. She suffers from a dichotomy between the split of life and love from death. By knowing she has reached full-circle, Djuna can confront illusory images that evade her memory. Closing the circle involves moving past the self-image of her father's "mystical bride," while allowing epiphanies to tend to Djuna's own sexuality, fear, sense of abandonment, and finally feelings of repulsion.

Winter of Artifice opens as Djuna awaits the return of her father after 20 years. This meeting is referenced as exemplifying "the circle of empty waiting [coming] to a close" (*Winter of Artifice* 55). The image that captures the cycle of beginning a love, the "passion," is "a glass bowl with the glass fish and the glass ship," representing the sea Djuna traveled, aboard a ship, carrying her away from her father "after he had abandoned her" (*Winter of Artifice* 55). The ship, the beginning of the sense of dualism that Djuna suffers, is linked to a sequence of lifelong events. The fragile glass containing the ship points to the possibility of escaping trauma and fear encircled around her father. For once the bowl "crack[s]" there is hope that she will reach the "end of [her] wandering" (*Winter of Artifice* 69).[4] The protagonist associates the ship with a perpetual sense of restlessness, as she ponders: "Why has she loved ships so deeply, why has she always wanted to sail away from this world?" (*Winter of Artifice* 55). Yet, on that day, with the arrival of her father, her disquiet state will reach new shores of understanding. But first, she must confront the "masks," "illusion," "dualism" and repulsion that propels her newly found perception of her father. Central to Djuna's conflict is how to commune with her father so as to obliterate the "confusion in her between god and father." I will return to this point shortly.

A reference to *Winter of Artifice* in Nin's *Incest: From a Journal of Love* is found in a diary entry dated February 4, 1934:

> I worked on three stories at once. Every day at *les Marronniers*, I wrote a few pages of the June-Henry novel, the final version ["Djuna"]. If in a mad, neurotic mood, obsessed, I wrote in "Alraune," adding diseased and monstrous pages. Whenever I returned from Father's, I added a few pages to "The Double," a story which Rank nurtured and inspired by his insight into the drama*.
>
> (The footnote states: *" 'Alraune' was an early version of *House of Incest*, and 'The Double' became the title story of the volume *Winter of Artifice*.")
>
> (*Incest* 304–305)

Early in the novel, the motif of a "double" serves as a guiding force of the duality that Djuna explores, as reflected first in Nin's diary. In the novel, the role of Djuna's diary is pivotal in recording her colorful and trickster imagination: "In this record which she faithfully kept for twenty years she spoke of her diary as her shadow, her double . . . As far as she knew this double was the diary which was full of reflections, like a mirror, which could change shape and color and serve all kinds of imaginative substitutions" (*Winter of Artifice* 66). Here the narrator voices the shape shifting, inherently trickster qualities of the diary, compounding the theme of the plain title of the novel, *Winter of Artifice*. Winter is the archetypal icy-cold season permeated by deception and duplicity that Djuna awakens to. This includes an awakening to the inner structures that hold false premises, which will lead to purging her of a fervid need for a father and god.

In an entry dated July 11, 1933 Nin references her diary as her "double," symbol of "self-love" (*Incest* 221). She goes on to question her reliance on her diary/double as a sign of weakness to engage in life: "Is it lack of resistance to the difficulties and pains of life with the Other – the Thous – *le Toi*? Is it always the moi – my Father, the male of me?" (*Incest* 221). Here, Nin makes a clear association with the diary as a place to divulge all that is associated with her father, both metaphorically and literally, including the parts of herself that she rejects. We are reminded that the association with her father as "the male of [her]" carries incestuous suggestions in metaphorical terms. We are also reminded of the dilemma of communion with self and artist that she grappled with throughout her life. Indeed, it was later that year, in November 1933, that Rank would advise Nin to "give up [her] diary" to focus solely on writing fiction (*Incest* 294). Moreover, the context for calling the diary her "double" seems to have been prompted by Rank's idea that Nin had "written the diary in order to replace [her] father, unconsciously imitating [her] father, too, and identifying [herself] with him" (*Incest* 298). To this Nin responds: "Diary then originates in the need to cover a loss, to fill a vacancy. I call the diary, little by little, a personage; then I confuse it with the shadow, *mon ombre* (my Double!) whom I am going to marry" (*Incest* 298). This reference to being a bride to her double is explored through the image of the mystical bride in the novel, to which I examine later in this chapter. Nin would continue finding a way to fill the "vacancy" in the process of writing about complex relationships, including the selfhood of the artist.

In *Incest: From a Journal of Love*, an entry dated May 5, 1933, Nin records the difference between her expectations of what her father would look like after 20 years and the man she actually meets in person: "I expected the man of the photographs, a face – less furrowed, less carved, more transparent. I found it so heavily engraved, stony, and at the same moment I liked the new face" (*Incest* 154–155). The description connotes the engraving of a "stony" face that is brought forth from the gaps of her memory. Yet, there is a "moment" of fresh perception of the "new face" detailed in facial features, including the "power" of particular characteristics. This emotional description is followed by a reference to her father as "My Double! My evil Double! He incarnates my fears, my self doubts, my faults . . . I am finished with any ideal image of myself. Father still carries this image" (*Incest* 155). Nin characterizes her father through the metaphor of incest by projecting the narcissism and weakness she finds in herself onto her father, as if they are one and the same human being. In the novel, however, the incongruity in his appearance and Djuna's own perception of her father persists, but a mask is used as a central metaphor. When Djuna sees her father, she remarks: "[his face] was not any older, there were no wrinkles on it, but there was a mask over it. His face wore a mask. The skin did not match the skin of his wrists. It seemed made of earth and papier-mache, not pure skin" (*Winter of Artifice* 67). Djuna doubts her father is made of human flesh when likening his skin to the fragility and flimsiness of paper. It is in this duplicitous world populated by masked beings that Djuna learns how to navigate her fantasies and multiplicitous sense of self. For central to Djuna's conflict is knowing how to "disentangle their two selves" (*Winter of Artifice* 92).

Nin's *Incest: From a Journal of Love* diary, published posthumously, records a climatic sexual encounter with her father as discussed in Chapter 4. It is the pivotal moment in the narrative wherein Nin makes herself utterly desirable to her father who then "penetrate[s] her three and four times without pausing and without withdrawing – his new strength, new desire" (*Incest* 212). At the end of this scene, Nin remembers her father uttering the words: "*Je n'ai plus de Dieu*! – I have lost God" (*Incest* 212). Here I'd like to revisit what I posited in Chapter 4, wherein I recall that Rank's understanding, which Nin was also prone to expounding, that engaging in a mythical account in "action and experience," and in Nin's case recording an embodied fantasy, preoccupied Nin at the time. In this representation, I have already suggested the parallels Nin drew between her incest narrative and the mythic story captured in the painting *Lot and His Daughters*. This incestuous reference is echoed in *Winter of Artifice*, as the communion that ensues is likened to a mystical experience.

In the novel, the "disentanglement" between Djuna and her father happens in the form of an intimacy separate of physical union. For example, following her father's declaration: "You are the synthesis of all the women I loved," the two listen to an orchestra "inside both their heads" (*Winter of Artifice* 84). It was an orchestra of "a hundred instruments playing all at once" (84). Both Djuna and her father embody the "strings . . . inside their bodies" (84). There are erotic references to "passing the violin bow gently between her legs, drawing music out of her body, her body foaming, the harp singing god . . . tears, through subterranean roads" (85). A narrative of stream of conscious erotic images evokes a transcendent awakening. For Djuna, the progression of time seems to shift: "everything lived out simultaneously, the love, the impulse, the doubt of the love, the knowledge of the love's death, the love of life, the doubt, the ecstasy, the knowledge of its death germ, everything like an orchestra" (88). To this she interjects the question: "Can we feel in rhythm, my father? Can we think in rhythm, my father? Rhythm – rhythm-rhythm" (88). The ravishing of music through a rapid rhythm is likened to a mystical union denoting the state of souls living intimately through harmony, grace and love. This scene is followed by a reference to an "ancient bridal canopy," and to Djuna as "The mystical bride of her father" (88–89). Djuna brings her mystical longing and mystery to an end. The dualism, including the split between temporal and eternal, the outer and the inner, matter and spirit, is resolved through the allusion of the mystical marriage. It is the mystical marriage archetype, after all, that inspires the soul's sacred journey toward the divine. But first the divine wedding is a mystery projected outside oneself. In Djuna's life, she has projected that love onto her father and those who resemble him. Nin emphasizes the bride of God, the mystical marriage, as a metaphor for a psychological reality that turns a new self-directed Eros toward Djuna herself.

Confirmation of Djuna's capacity to extricate herself from the illusion and suffering of dualism occurs in a scene toward the conclusion of the novel. Djuna detects new details in her father; "through this mask of coldness which had terrified her as a child she was better able as a woman to detect the malady of his soul. His soul was sick" (94). Djuna meets the revelation of her father's diseased soul with utter disgust. The epiphany results in the loss of faith in her father, specifically when "they looked at each other across miles and miles of separation. Their eyes did not meet. His fear of emotion enwrapped him in glass. This glass shut out the warmth of life, its human odors" (94). The image of the father and daughter separated by a glass division suggests a greenhouse deprived of the "warmth of life," once again evoking the title of an icy *Winter of Artifice*.

In the concluding scene of the novel, Djuna realizes her adherence to a "pattern" not set in reality. Only then is she able to make an emotional break from her father. Djuna understands the mystical union is the true "fulfillment," as there is no need for incestuous love with her father to be literalized. In the next scene, Djuna enters "the Chinese theater of her drama and could see the trappings of the play as well as the play itself, see that the settings were made of the cardboard of illusion" (118–119). Djuna walks "behind the stage" and sees that the "suffering was no longer real" (119). Finally, at that moment, Djuna feels as if she is "coming out of the ether of the past," as a metaphor for having felt captured in an insensitive and oblivious world of the past.[5]

In *The Novel of the Future*, Nin points out that "in *Winter of Artifice* I wanted to express the daughter's desire to be very close to her father, as close and as intimate as a daughter and father might be without sexual union. Emotional harmony and intimacy which are not literal incest" (30). It is clear that Nin was aware of the risk involved in pursuing incest themes. She goes on to explain: "Such a close scrutiny of a relationship between father and daughter risks being misunderstood, as so many unconscious drives are, except by the analyst. Unconsciously, certainly, the daughter seeks a form of union while respecting taboos" (*Novel of the Future* 30). It is important to note that Nin's reflection on the mystical engagement between father and daughter is revelatory and consistent to the audacity required to write a diary like Journal Book 42, included in *Incest: From a Journal of Love*. Nin held true to an artistic credo positing that taboos in life are not exempt from literary exploration, especially within a literary milieu like the 1920s and 1930s.

Conclusion: rounding and polishing of an unexpurgated self

The biographical outline in *Winter of Artifice* is evident: dualism between life and death, fantasies and anxieties with father-God image, Oedipal violence, the repetition of destructive patterns resulting in co-dependency of others, and making sense of multiple selves amidst a disintegrating world. These are all themes which Nin first explored in diary writing, as they also remained central to her poetic prose of the 1930s and 1940s. Her literary diary was a place to make narrative and poetic sense of her creativity – a "human document" from which to create a myth of her own.

In *Incest: From a Journal of Love*, as shown here, Nin documents personas born of fragments within fantasies and psychological realities that in *Winter of Artifice* reveal symbolic, poetic and mythic structures of psyche. Nin openly shared that it was her diary writing that fostered her development of metaphors for psychic states of mind later developed in her fiction, as imagined in *Winter of Artifice*. My close reading, though of select passages, hopes to invite more extensive readings in concert of these literary works. It is through close and critical reading of these texts, along with the literary and cultural context of the time, that will encourage new generations to bring Nin's literary achievements out of the polemic and into the spirit of revival.

Notes

1 See Otto Rank's work *Art and Artist: Creative Urge and Personality Development* wherein he studies the artist, creative process and society.

2 This, along with Nin's other diaries, are housed in the UCLA archives, which I had access to.

3 See Nalbantian's chapter "The Mythification of Selfhood in Anaïs Nin," where she expounds on Nin's artistic transposition of father/daughter relationships in her fiction. This essay is in *Aesthetic Autobiography: From Life to Art in Marcel Proust, James Joyce, Virginia Woolf and Anaïs Nin.*

4 In her study of *Winter of Artifice*, Bettina L. Knapp analyzes the optical illusions reflected in the objects as symbolic of Djuna's conflict. See *Anaïs Nin*, p. 78.

5 Nalbantian's study of this scene in "The Mythification of Selfhood in Anaïs Nin" includes references to Nin's linking of metaphor with real life experiences to compound Djuna's experiences. This essay is in *Aesthetic Autobiography: From Life to Art in Marcel Proust, James Joyce, Virginia Woolf and Anaïs Nin*, p. 182.

Works cited

Didion, Joan. *The White Album*. New York: Simon and Schuster. 1979. Print.

Hinz, Evelyn J. Ed. *A Woman Speaks: The Lectures, Seminars, and Interviews of Anaïs Nin*. Chicago: Swallow Press. 1975. Print.

Nalbantian, Suzanne. *Aesthetic Autobiography: From Life to Art in Marcel Proust, James Joyce, Virginia Woolf and Anaïs Nin*. New York: St. Martin's Press. 1994. Print.

Nin, Anaïs. *Winter of Artifice*. Chicago: Swallow Press. 1945. Print.

———. *Seduction of the Minotaur*. Athens: Ohio UP. 1961. Print.

———. *D. H. Lawrence: An Unprofessional Study*. Chicago: Swallow Press. 1964. Print.

———. *The Novel of the Future*. New York: Collier Books. 1968. Print.

———. *The Diary of Anaïs Nin Volume One (1931–1934)*. New York: Harvest. 1969a. Print.

———. *The Diary of Anaïs Nin Volume Four (1944–1947)*. New York: Harvest. 1969b. Print.

———. *Incest: From a Journal of Love (1932–1934)*. New York: Harcourt Brace Jovanovich. 1992. Print.

Rank, Otto. *Art and Artist: Creative Urge and Personality Development*. New York: W.W. Norton. 1932. Print.

Chapter 6

Myth, monsters and art

The labyrinths of Nin's *Seduction of the Minotaur*

> Myth is at the beginning of literature, and also at its end.
>
> (Jorge Luis Borges 1964)

In this chapter, I show how Nin rewrites the minotaur myth in *Seduction of the Minotaur*, published in 1961, the final novelette in the five-part series, *Cities of the Interior*, to allegorically chronicle the protagonist Lillian Beye's underworld journey. Lillian draws from resources linked to earth-mother consciousness, including an innate understanding of her own sensory traces in her body. As I noted in Chapter 1, earth-mother consciousness proposes the instinct for relationship and meaning, "based on the principle of the relationship of the manifest to the unmanifest" (Baring, Cashford 159). I wish to place emphasis on Lillian's unfolding journey as it is symbolic of a *nykeia*, the archetypal journey which integrates the unconscious parts of her psyche.[1] Of particular importance is the effect of corporeal gender on Lillian's *nykeia* experience. By suggesting that biological gender does indeed shape psyche, Nin reveals an ontological understanding of recovering the embodied feminine psyche.

To better understand how Nin turns around the minotaur myth in her novelette, it is first important to recall the ruling Greek minotaur myth. It is also valuable to know that all such mythological stories both evoke mystery and vary in details depending on the narrator. The basic classic Greek myth of Theseus and the minotaur recounts a tale in which Minos, King of Crete, orders Daedalus to construct at Knossos a maze, the labyrinth, in which to conceal the minotaur, a monster, half man and half bull, who is destined to feed upon seven youths and seven maidens sacrificed annually. Theseus, the national hero of Athens, voluntarily joins the fourteen youths and maidens sent as tribute. Theseus enters the labyrinth and reaches the center by following the string that Ariadne, daughter of Minos, extends, suggesting a retracing of the umbilical link to the womb where mysteries of the Goddess reside. He kills the minotaur and finds his way back out of the underworld maze, into the upper world, by means of the same thread Ariadne offered. Ariadne then falls in love with Theseus and he agrees to marry her. Later, however, he betrays Ariadne and abandons her on the island of Naxos;

he is cosmically punished when he returns to Athens, for by failing to raise the white sail of victory, he causes his father's suicide. Theseus later marries Ariadne's sister Phaedra, but he is again punished for his betrayal when Phaedra falsely accuses his son Hippolytus of raping her.

The Greek minotaur mythology has undergone a process of revision, unsurprisingly, since it is a myth that was "the first story we have of Crete, even though it is told 1,000 years later from a perspective of a culture much changed from the original one" (Baring 137). This myth was painted on Greek vases dating from the eighth century BC onwards, and was written down by Homer, Hesiod, Thucydides, Pindar, Plutarch and Ovid (Baring 137). This myth, according to Baring and Cashford's research, focuses on Theseus as the Greek hero myth, in which Theseus slays the monster in the dark underground labyrinth and wins freedom for his country. Although it is important that a possible historical truth to the story comes through the perspective of a different culture: "the tribute of seven youths and seven maidens whom the Athenians were bound to send to Minos every eight years had some connection with the renewal of the king's power for another cycle" (Baring 139). Myths contain mysteries and often ambiguities that invite us to raise questions. In literature, myths are poeticized. Mythological imagery gives literary works form and meaning as they are at the root of knowing and guide the human imagination.

The ancient minotaur myth (along with a fascination with monsters and human nature) has had a persistent presence in literature and art. Therefore, it is essential to contextualize Nin's own interest in the mythological beast. Fast-forwarding to the 19th century, an important literary depiction of the creation of a monster and its subsequent representations is Mary Shelley's *Frankenstein*, published in 1818. Marian Warner's analysis of Mary Shelley's work, recounted in her essay "Boys Will Be Boys," examines how Mary Shelley portrays monsters based on the depiction of Frankenstein's creation. Warner illuminates the figurative creation of monsters as a metaphor for the psychological management of our fears and anxieties. In her analysis Warner argues, "Mary Shelley grasped the likelihood that a man might make a monster in his own image and then prove incapable of taking responsibility for him" (2). A close reading of the creator's response provides us with an alternative model by which to respond to the monsters. For example, Frankenstein's monster asks that Dr. Frankenstein remember that "I am thy creature, and I will be even mild and docile to my natural lord and king if thou wilt also perform thy part, which thou owes me" (Warner 29). Shelley's novel pleads on behalf of the monster that he be loved, not abandoned. In contrast to Theseus' method, Shelley's viewpoint is opposed to dealing with evil through heroic and lethal means. Instead, Shelley "recasts" the monster as his creator, "who acts to define him" (Warner 3). Nin also supposed that monsters in myth have something profound to reveal about the dualities that compel the creator/artist to make unconscious fears conscious.

The literary re-visionings of the minotaur myth in the 20th century provides a window into the fear and anxiety of the prevalent time. In the 1930s there is a resurgence of the minotaur in Europe when the catastrophe of Europe's wars, civil wars and economic depressions weighed on the minds of men and women in European society. In his excellent study *Minos and the Moderns: Cretan Myth in Twentieth-Century Literature and Art*, Theodore Ziolkowski argues that "as the thickening clouds of dictatorship and war darkened Europe's cultural landscape in the 1930s, the effect was rapidly apparent in the use of classical images" (67). One other contributing catalyst was the publication of the six volumes of the *Palace of Minos* (1921–1935), "in which Sir Arthur Evans described the results of his spectacular excavations in Knossos, the site of the tale" (70). These new insights led artists to speculate on the history of the minotaur (70). In fact, the 1930s led to the creation of the surrealist-oriented journal *Le Minotaure*, replete with many artistic renditions of various aspects of the myth on the covers. In addition, the minotaur became a central theme in the 1930s in paintings by Andre Masson, obsessed with what he noted was "the idea that Europe was on the point of being consumed by fire and blood" (74).

Pablo Picasso too joined the ranks of artists for whom the minotaur captured fears and anxieties of the collective psyche. The minotaur is the principle theme in Picasso's work from 1933 to 1936, in a series of five etchings entitled, *Minotauros with a Dagger* (one of these sketches was used for the collage on the cover of the first issue of *Le Minotaur*) (Ziolkowski 75). The minotaur was also a central figure in Picasso's "Guernica," famously depicting the carnage of the Spanish Civil War. A decade later, in South America, in his short story, "The House of Asterion," published in 1947, Jorge Luis Borges considers the minotaur myth from the perspective of the minotaur. In Borges' story, the minotaur does not see himself as a prisoner, for "there are no locks on the doors" (Borges 139). Yet he does not make his way into the light. The minotaur, instead of a monstrosity, yearns to see himself as kind. He considers himself a liberator of the nine men that visit him every "nine years so that they can be redeemed" (140). Borges depicts a minotaur with a vulnerable and innocent side that invokes sympathy from the reader. Again the following decade, the surrealist artist Leonora Carrington, painting in New York in 1953, created *And Then We Saw the Daughters of the Minotaur*. Carrington captures a white minotaur clothed in a red robe. It resembles a horse, not a bull. Nonetheless, the minotaur holds court while apparitions dance in the air. A goddess casts enchantment on the entire room. The two young girls dressed in black robes watch in amazement, in a serene and mysterious scene.

It is through such fictional and artistic representations that the minotaur myth survived metaphorically across the decades in various works, not the least Nin's *Seduction of the Minotaur*, published in 1961. In my analysis of this work, I demonstrate the thematic ways that Nin contends myth in literature define enemies – adversaries – as well as the ways to confront social and personal ills in society.

Seducing the minotaur

Each of the five novelettes of *Cities of the Interior* was published individually during the 1940s and 1950s. It was not until after Nin's diaries were published beginning in 1966 that these novels received greater attention, for it was only following the publication of Nin's diaries that the novelettes were published together under the single title of *Cities of the Interior*. *Seduction of the Minotaur* portrays the protagonist Lillian's journey that leads to a level of elevated self-awareness by penetrating her labyrinth, the unconscious. She draws from past memories, embodied experiences with nature and a self-directed Eros that leads to transformation.

Lillian travels to tropical Golconda, Mexico, a place that will be her link to the tender voices within her own psyche, to inspire union of nature, body and soul. The opening passage of the novel frames the source of Lillian's desires as originating in the unconscious, a dream:

> Some voyages have their inception in the blueprint of a dream, some in the urgency of contradicting a dream. Lillian's recurrent dream of a ship that could not reach the water, that sailed laboriously, pushed by her with great effort, through city streets, had determined her course toward the sea, as if she would give this ship once and for all, its proper sea bed.
>
> (5)

In this lucid opening, the reader is situated in the heart of the dream that guides Lillian's journey. We immediately learn that Lillian is being propelled by a voice of intuition and creativity that sets up an archetypal position to pursue her freedom. The "course towards the sea" sets a rhythm for Lillian's journey. Yet her demons must be pursued, and like Theseus's willingness to move through the labyrinth, Lillian too will move through hers. However, in contrast to the original classical Greek myth, I argue that without the lethal deed (using a sword), Lillian's process of slaying her figurative demons involves responses to the call of giving the "ship once and for all, its proper seabed," symbolic of an inner need to liberate herself as a woman. Lillian is buoyed by both water and earth; she journeys towards more than adventure, but also the dangers of life. What is more, Lillian's experiences have roots in the oceans of the origin of life associated with the birth of Aphrodite, the Greek Goddess of beauty and love. Early in this novel Lillian must return to the original ocean as a source of creation, as I explore later in this chapter.

The tropical setting of Golconda vivifies Lillian's journey towards a richer and more integrated life; however, initially, her desire to embark on her own *nykeia* journey is limited to the realm of her unconscious. Upon her first breaths of fresh air in Golconda, we learn that Lillian "inhaled a drug of forgetfulness known to adventurers" (5). Lillian reflects: "I came here to forget myself" (47). It is only when Lillian discards illusions of her life that she realizes that "the voyage underground had taken longer, and had taken her farther" (90).

Lillian comes to Golconda from an otherwise sterile world that bears little connection to nature or to the physical body, for early in the novel the reader learns that "where Lillian came from people seemed intent on not seeing each other, and against improvisation" (6–7). Nin's female protagonist reminds us that society assigns culturally constructed meaning to gender that is encumbered with duties of caring and nurturing others' interest, ultimately making women incapable of forming their own experiences. Indeed, within the first 10 pages of the novel, we learn that Lillian's observations of Golconda are tampered with by the three men in a taxi trying to prevent her ability to form her own opinion of the city, as they unwelcoming offer their subjective and authoritative experiences. As she listens, Lillian reveals feeling "that these three men were somehow interfering with her own tasting of Golconda. They seemed intent on giving her an image of Golconda she did not want" (10).

The landscape, as the backdrop for Lillian's voyage inward, is dominated by the color gold. In alchemic traditions gold is connected to the sun, unveiling what is hidden in the womb of Mother Earth. The narrator draws us into Golconda by remarking: Lillian "landed in the city of Golconda, where the sun painted everything with gold, the lining of her thoughts, the worn valise, . . . the golden aster, the golden eagle, the golden goose, the golden fleece, the golden robin, the goldenrod, the goldenseal, the golden warbler, the golden wattles" (5). This *rubedo* world becomes the physical place where a transformation of raw emotional material will unfold.

While Western alchemic tradition is known as the process that turns lead into gold, in our current scientific age we now regard the role of alchemy in the mythic imagination. It is useful to consider the link between the psyche and body of the alchemist connecting to nature in a sacred act of making art (gold) (*The Ecocritical Psyche* 29). The process of creating gold in Western alchemic traditions has metaphoric associations with the process of birth and decay. Hence, the creation of gold can be linked to new life emerging from the indigenous psyche. In her own understanding of alchemy, Nin was aware of the alchemist's potential for transmutation, as Bettina Knapp points out in her study *Anaïs Nin*. Knapp writes, "Nin had learned much from the research work she had done for Dr. Allendy, particularly in the realm of alchemy, and she became fascinated by the psychological as well as by the artistic approach to this science" (60). In *Seduction of the Minotaur*, gold symbolizes illumination and an ability to engage in the transformation process. The ultimate phase of the alchemical process is to rid the impurities and transform the *prima materia* into gold. The Philosopher's Stone is created by joining the opposites (Knapp 66).

In *Seduction of the Minotaur*, the foreshadowing of Lillian's efforts towards transformation is seen early in the novel, as the reader is introduced to Lillian in the golden-bathed Golconda. Soon after arriving in Golconda, "already she felt incarnated, in full possession of her own body because the porter was in full possession of his, and this concentration upon the present allowed no interruption or short circuits of the physical contact" (7). Lillian envelops herself in a golden and sacred setting that will help propel her, as she draws closer to an embodied spirit that lies within herself.

Consequently, the nature of Lillian's descent puts her into contact with feminine mysteries and paradoxes. I am not suggesting that the underworld is a feminine place in an essentialist sense. For example, we know that Persephone's abduction is by Hades, and it is he who initiates Persephone into the underworld. Rather, I am pointing to the ways in which bodily form experiences the psyche in gender-specific ways. Here, I agree with Rowland's notion that men and women "may experience the underworld differently through their bodies, while also being able to psychically imagine themselves in the body of the other" (*The Ecocritical Psyche* 167). By using myth as a "narrative vehicle" we can better understand that Lillian's *nykeia* experience is feminine in the way that she grapples and works towards making it possible to relate to all parts of her (*The Ecocritical Psyche* 167). She will travel below the golden sunlit landscape of Golconda, where "thoughts and memories which the air, the scents, and the music conspired to hypnotize by softness" (6). Lillian descends into the depths of her own darkness, and learns how to be in relationship with it in order to recreate her life.

Early in the novel, Lillian is given the clues toward unlocking human paradoxes and possible depths that must be traversed for transformation. Dr. Hernandez, sagaciously speaking about psychological patterns pursued in life says, "and one day we open our eyes, and there we are caught in the same pattern, repeating the same story. How could it be otherwise? The design comes from within us. It is internal" (19). The probing of this internal design is linked to an underworld journey through Lillian's past.

Moreover, in the novel, a catalyst for Lillian's epiphany is her confrontation with mortality when Dr. Hernandez's life tragically ends. To this event, Lillian responds: "If only Doctor Hernandez had not postponed that deeper, wilder talk which ran underground through the myths of dreams" (95). A confrontation with death urges Lillian to risk breaking the familiar deadening ways of relational patterns. To deepen her understanding of that "preciousness" of life, Lillian must excavate the depths of her psyche. The "dangers of disappearance" are near, and Lillian's response to death is life; one way for her to pursue life is to contend with that which must die from her past. It is Dr. Hernandez who instructs Lillian about the role of memory and psyche in obtaining psychological wholeness when he claims: "Some memories are imbedded in the flesh like splinters . . . and you have to operate to get them out" (28). The surgical removal of such traumatic memories is a way of handling the past that Lillian will have to embrace. Thus, Lillian's psyche is stirred through emotions and sensations that help those memories emerge.

In her study *Memory of Literature: From Rousseau to Neuroscience*, Suzanne Nalbantian characterizes Nin's exploration of memory in *Seduction of the Minotaur* as a place where "Nin constructs an archaeology of memory" (118). Nalbantian writes:

> For Nin, the image of the labyrinth represents the brain in its intricate layers of memory circuits, comparable to what the British neurologist Tim Shallice has called "nested structures." Her locales are often transformed into an inner space, which she inhabits through the power of memory. Passages such as tunnels, grooves, corridors, mazes in underground cities are the networks through which memories pass through the strata of consciousness.
>
> (118–119)

Nalbantian analyzes Lillian's ability to access and understand her short-term, as well as long-term, memories, which ultimately help Lillian face the mystery of her own labyrinth. Nalbantian sees the journey through darkness as a path to Lillian's past, and it is through sensory signs that Lillian retrieves her deepest memories. For example, when Lillian meets Hatcher, an American engineer and longtime resident of Mexico, her eyes meet his hands and she observes that he had "hair on his fingers, like her father" (75). By invoking the "emotional brain" Nin "conveys the memory process in terms of her own footsteps which trace these grooves" (Nalbantian 121). Another important visual cue that evokes Lillian's memory is when she sees a six-year old child in the plane (*Seduction* 121). This image, "carried [Lillian] by a detour into the past, to a certain day in her childhood, in Mexico, where her father frustrated by enigmatic natives, and elemental cataclysms, would come home to the one kingdom, at least, where his will was unquestioned" (*Seduction* 111). The recollection of her commanding and calculating father involves, as Nalbantian explains, a "strange mixture of pain and pleasure hence, a sensory trace is part of this memory" (121). Lillian recalls another pivotal childhood memory of her abusive father:

> He would receive from the mother a report. And no matter how mild she made this, how much she attenuated the children's infractions, the father always found the cause enough to march them up to the top floor, an attic filled with dusty objects. And there, one by one, he spanked them.
>
> (111)

Consequently, Lillian is able to return to the harrowing memories of her violent father as a way to begin the purging process needed to heal old wounds. For Nin, we are reminded, memories in fiction serve the potential for "living moments" taken from the quotidian of the character's life. Nin reflects on her method of using memories as heightened psychological moments when writing: "a living emotion is captured without dying in the process is a mystery unless one accepts that to translate a living emotion into words, the emotion must be strong enough to survive the transplantation" (*The Novel of the Future* 57). The strength behind her protagonist's emotional experiences are evoked through memories, in this specific instance, of terror of a dominating father. Nalbantian remarks that *Seduction of the Minotaur* is akin to a "modern myth of memory in the figure of the minotaur" (119). Indeed, Nin admitted that one role of her fiction is "the creation of the myth" (*Novel of the Future* 158). Furthermore, Nin's revision of the minotaur myth is both a modern and ancient myth of memory, which reveals Nin's method of using metaphors, myths and archetypes to reshape literary forms as a Modernist.

The autobiographical content of *Seduction of the Minotaur* is evident. Lillian, like Nin, makes efforts toward escaping from a complicated attachment to her father. Nin had a lifelong struggle with coming to terms with her father's abuse, as well as abandonment of the family in 1913, which is the catalyst for her first diary of 1914. When Nin's father died in October 1949, in a diary entry, Nin writes: "Why did he build a wall around himself? Why did he always seek the flaws in others, why were his blue eyes so critical? . . . He was full of aesthetic admiration for his children. It was the only moment in which he showed interest" (5:51). In Nin's diary, memories of her father are linked to the metaphor of a wall built around himself to distance his contact with his children, as if fearing their devouring nature. The image of a self-imposed labyrinth is given a fresh perspective in the novel through Lillian's own experiences with past memories of her distant and abusive father. Lillian, like Nin the artist, is on a journey to invent a fresh vision of herself absent her father's critical gaze. In the novel, the need to escape an abusive father is expressed through figurative expression which reference that "children do not possess eyes of their own." Rather, children see themselves through the eyes of their parents (*Seduction of the Minotaur* 85). In these passages, Nin takes the fragments of memories of the psychological reality of a father's confused adoration for his children and reorders them in the novel through aesthetic metaphors.

Nalbantian's analysis of the memory circuitry as a part of a complex labyrinth further helps to understand how Nin weaves Ariadne's myth into this exquisite novel. It is Ariadne, after all, who, through her strategic plan, becomes the mistress of the labyrinth. In the Greek minotaur myth, it is she who devises the plan, together with Daedalus, to help Theseus escape the labyrinth using her ball of thread. As perceptively noted by Nalbantian, "Language is Ariadne's thread which retraces the footsteps of imprints, physically designed within the intricacies of the labyrinth" (118). Also, in her study of Ariadne, in *Pagan Grace*, as a "crafty heroine," Ginette Paris posits that, "Theseus's type of courage, needed to kill the Minotaur, is no help in this context. It takes the genius of Ariadne, the crafty heroine, who anticipates, consults, takes it over, and comes up with a simple, creative idea that resolves the most incredible confused situation" (43). When considering Nin's fascination with and artistic mastery over language, and her reliance on language to orient herself in complex and potentially overwhelming life experiences, it is fitting that Nin's reworking is from Ariadne's perspective. In the novel, it is Ariadne's thread that guides Lillian through the darkness, as the narrator reflects: "It was a night journey into the past, and the thread that had pulled her was one of accidental resemblances, familiarity, the past" (75).

Immediately following her interaction with Hatcher, and his hands that resemble her father's, Lillian engages sensory clues from nature. While walking on the beach, Lillian set eyes on the "open" and "violet red velvety faces" of the flowers. Following this enveloping and "folding" like "layers" in the sea, Lillian feels herself becoming one of the red flowers. The tension in Lillian's body dissolves and emotions circulate freely (78). Through an embodied experience, self-directed Eros emerges. It is obvious that Lillian is not experiencing the mythic energy of one who conquers, such as Theseus, but rather faces the feelings of renewal and emergences in a sacred bath. These images also evoke the realm of Aphrodite. It is Aphrodite after all who reminds us that the origin of all life resides in the depths of the sea.

One pre-patriarchal myth of Aphrodite's birth tells us that she was born from the sea-foam. It is worth directly quoting this version of the myth as retold by Ginette Paris in *Pagan Grace*:

> Life was young and frail when Aphrodite arose with the breath of renewal. Borne by gentle winds on the eastern sea, she alighted on the island of Cyprus. So graceful and alluring was the Goddess that the Seasons rushed to meet her, imploring her always to stay. Aphrodite smiled. Her stay would be never-ending, her work never complete . . . She blessed the females' wombs, guarded them as they grew, and warded off lover's pains at birth. Everywhere, Aphrodite drew forth the hidden promise of life. Every day she kissed the earth with morning dew. The wanderings of the Goddess carried her far, yet each spring she returned with her doves to Cyprus for her sacred bath at Paphos . . . Aphrodite walked into the sea, into the pulsing moon rhythms of the tide. When she emerged with her spirit renewed, spring blossomed fully and all beings felt her joy. Through seasons, years, eras, Aphrodite's mysteries remain inviolable, for she alone understands the love that begets life.
>
> (Paris 12–13)

This mystery of Aphrodite alludes to the possibilities of a sensory rebirth and renewal by embracing a sacred bath to renew the spirit. Lillian gives precedence to the feminine Aphrodite mode of thought. When she steps out of the sea "and put on her clothes she felt reborn, born anew" (78). It is in a state of mystery and remembering that Lillian understands the importance of a self-directed Eros to help propel her through psychic depths, for "the farther she traveled into unknown places, unfamiliar places, the more precisely she could find within herself a map showing only the cities of the interior" (80). It is by exploring the metaphorical cities of her interior heart and soul that Lillian can encounter the minotaur.

It is as if, in the expansive and flowering archetypal mystery of Aphrodite, Lillian is subsequently able to explore a new level of self-understanding that implements the knowledge and wisdom symbolic of a confrontation with the minotaur. Her journey inward now allows Lillian to view others more transparently. She confesses: "I can see that it is in this distorted vision of the world's proper proportions that lies the secret of our fears" (88). Assuming this sensibility, Lillian's remembrances of her mother are evoked; the narrator remarks: "She remembered that her mother never had a wrinkle on her dress, or a lock of hair out of place, and was always putting on her gloves as if she were a noted surgeon about to operate" (88). Lillian considers the effect distorted images of her mother had on their relationship. Amid this insight, Lillian no longer sees her mother through the lens of a child, and from the perspective of an adult woman, she is better equipped to explore this troubled relationship as another defective pattern in her own life. Following her mother's death, "Lillian became her mother for at least a long year of mourning" (120). She blames her culture for the lack of ritualized ways of honoring and embracing mortality (120). Suffering from projections on her mother, and when she inherits a "thimble, and a sewing machine (when Lillian could not sew) Lillian did not know that she took on some of her moods, characteristics, attitudes" (101). It is through the related objects that Lilian finds herself becoming absorbed in the traits exhibited by her mother. Lillian understands that in grieving the loss of her mother she can find freedom.

A diary entry dated August 1954, the year Nin's mother passed away, sheds light on what was preoccupying her while writing – one can say mothering – the novel *Seduction of the Minotaur*. Nin laments that with the end of her own mother's life comes the realization that "[her] hope of fulfillment, of union with her, of an understanding, penetrating love" is also forever lost (5:176). Nin reflects that the death of a mother became a profound void of "penetrating love." The death of a mother represents a universal crisis resulting from the loss of the giver of life, the female energy principle. This death alters the path of Nin's quotidian world. The items she inherits from her mother, such as "a gold thimble" and "the diaries she had bound by hand in France," symbolically link the two women together (5:182). These objects permeate Nin's life at the time, leaving her feeling "possessed" by her mother's spirit (5:182). Lillian, too, is overcome and in similar acts, she honors and grieves the loss of a mother. Furthermore, Nin's diary entry reflects her deeply emotional, conscious devotion and associations with the loss of her mother. She writes: "the pain deeper than at my father's death. I didn't love her well enough. Except from the age of eleven until twenty, when I was completely and utterly devoted to her, thinking only of helping her" (5:181). Grieving the loss of a mother who was the nucleus of her existence points to an archetypal predicament of man and woman that Lillian, in turn, experiences.

Before Lillian can create a new life, she must recognize that "the spirit of her mother had passed into her" (101). Similarly, in a diary entry that same year, Nin ponders a profound insight that "[i]n ancient mystic beliefs, the spirit of the dead entered a newborn child. Surely our parents give birth to us twice, the second time when they die, and as they die, in rebellion against death, we accept the legacy of their character traits" (5:184). Through the application of an ancient belief on mortality, in her fiction, Nin imbeds a collective experience to Lillian's personal universe. Also, Lillian's realization that she must create a new life, a new myth to guide her, is akin to Ariadne experiencing death of her old life and the need to create a new one. It is by better understanding her mother's memories through a "possession" that Lillian's soul recovers faith. Lillian sees through the labyrinths of her own self-sabotaging and destructive "design" (psychological patterns) to end the cycle.

This moment of self-reflection links Lillian to a healing process described through the image of the labyrinth. Lillian is better able to understand that the past is linked to the present, as a way to create a new mythology by which to live. She realizes that one's outer nature is linked to an interior reality. Here, Lillian is cultivating the aptitude to free herself from past wounds. Lillian empathizes that she must change for her relationship to "sustain the myth of freedom," by which she seems to mean free from her haunting past (109). Lillian's confrontation with her metaphorical minotaur frees not only herself, but also the individuals whose images are prisoners in her mind. This personal vision turns into a guide for the collective who also "meander labyrinths" and hold projections, as if keeping others prisoners in cells of our own remembering. Lillian's capability to release her illusions is captured in some of the most poetic prose of the entire novel, when the narrator celebrates:

> Lillian was journeying homeward. The detours of the labyrinth did not expose disillusion, but unexplored dimensions. Archeologists of the soul never returned empty handed. Lillian had felt the existence of the labyrinth beneath her feet like the excavated passageways under Mexico City, but she had feared entering it and meeting the Minotaur who would devour her.
>
> (111)

It is not until Lillian can come face-to-face with the minotaur that she can live more freely: "Yet now that she had come face-to-face with it, the minotaur resembled someone she knew. It was not a monster. It was a reflection upon a mirror, a masked woman" (111). Nin translates Lillian's restraint into suggestive awareness that leads to more self-acceptance. Lillian's spirit has been drawn to make the effort to live a more awakened life. She takes a spiritual journey through the labyrinth and encounters insight into a deeper way to live. Bettina Knapp explains Lillian's newly acquired capabilities by reflecting that: "She has found and established contact with the animal within her, the instinctual Dionysian realm. She has also understood the Apollonian, or the rational, aspect of life" (148). Indeed, it is through a newly acquired intimacy with the "animal within her," in an "instinctual Dionysian realm" that Lillian is able to celebrate a newly discovered Eros towards life that animates the inner-self. It is after all the exceptional gift of Dionysos that "is bursting energy that breaks through the tyranny of the ego which will allow only one kind of feeling, that breaks through the internalization of Pentheus's rules and Platonic devaluation of the feminine" (Paris 33). Embracing a Dionysian sensitivity further invites a receptive Lillian to be intimate with her intuitive nature.

Lillian's realization wonderfully fuses with Nin's own conscious understanding of how to balance the "outer and the inner," the past and present. Indeed, Nin reflects on her novel *Seduction of the Minotaur* with this insight: "The theme of the book itself is balance, balance between outer and inner, between past and present, between psychological reality and nature" (*Novel of the Future* 140). In the end, Lillian achieves this balance through the archetypal experiences of bodily and psychic integration. She is able to embrace the myth of her own life. Lillian is able to more richly engage in her life by considering the mythic mystery of living a purposeful life. The last sentence of *Seduction of the Minotaur* is evidence that Lillian integrates what is revealed to her on this *nykeia* journey. To conclude we learn: "In silence, in mystery, a human being was formed, was exploded, was struck by other passing bodies, was burned, was deserted. And then it was born in the molten love of the one who cared" (136). The journal entry that proceeds Nin's reflection on her personal mother reads: "I am at work on Lillian's return to her home and children, and in musical terms, Lillian is struggling with the muted tones she had not been able to hear" (5:184).

For Nin, the mythographer, myth informed consciousness, as well as made form out of consciousness. She underscored that there is a relationship between our inner experiences and those unfolding in nature as represented in the "outer journey" (*A Woman Speaks* 146). The archetype of an embodied journey toward insight, while guided by intuition, by one's own animal nature, bridges the relationship between somatic experience and myth. Nin's exploration of the enlightening possibilities of the body and psyche show us how to better understand balancing the outer and inner, body and nature.

What is fascinating about Nin's re-writing of the minotaur myth is the way a female heroine gives birth to a new sense of self. From the female narrator's point of view, we understand that Lillian's desire is to connect with the world of nature and the thresholds of the spiritual world. By traversing the wild feminine oceans, Lillian reaches the shores of understanding that death and disorder can hover always above the surface while she herself is pulled towards life. By evoking the Greek minotaur myth in the title of the novelette as the framework for building her story, Nin invites the reader into the realm of a transformative and mythic imaginings. In *Seduction of the Minotaur*, the reader moves into a narrative flow that unites with the reader's own psychic understanding of mighty monsters and labyrinths. Here the transformation of the Greek myth of the minotaur takes on new energy – a new, yet familiar, narrative. Nin uses myth, metaphors and *mimesis* to bind her literary work together into a spiritual journey of a confrontation with the shadows in the labyrinths of the unconscious as a way to better understand the indigenous psyche.

Conclusion: Theseus severs and Lillian intuits

In his book *Myth*, Laurence Coupe argues that a Jungian reading of the minotaur myth is that the labyrinth represents the unconscious (139). Coupe interprets Theseus' choice to abandon Ariadne to show the "reassertion of aggressive, male rationality, for which a price must be paid, symbolized by the violent end of both father and son" (139). Theseus takes the journey to the underworld and encounters the "shadow" (minotaur) under the inspiration of the anima (Ariadne). Theseus' neglect of Ariadne suggests that he will be unable to infuse feminine wisdom, including the ability to embrace self-Eros (139). In the end, Theseus manages to slay the minotaur, however, only to lose sight of the female wisdom that not only saved his life, but could have been gained during the journey.

Nin seems to suggests that slaying the monster with the energy and effort to conquer, as Theseus does, is not the only way to manage and vanquish the demons occupying psyche. By making Ariadne the protagonist, Nin suggests it is worthwhile exploring and embracing a *nykeia* journey from the feminine embodiment as ontologically powerful and going beyond what is commonly termed gender essentialism. By abandoning and exploiting Ariadne, (feminine) Theseus hence resigns the opportunity to internalize the emotional growth that is illuminated in the underworld. In Nin's rewriting of the myth, Lillian embraces her inner landscape, including living viscerally in nature, as a source of edification and courage to live more fully. Lillian explores "the detours of the labyrinth" knowing that they do "not expose disillusion, but unexplored dimension," which ultimately reveals feminine wisdom and new life (*Seduction* 111). Nin's powerful retelling of the myth of the minotaur as a feminine-embodied and spiritual journey reminds humanity that confronting and taming shadows is a necessity teeming with transformative energy.

Note

1 As referenced in Chapter 1, *nykeia* is a Homeric term for the descent to the underworld.

Works cited

Baring, Anne and Jules Cashford. *The Myth of the Goddess: Evolution of an Image*. New York: Penguin Books. 1991. Print.

Borges, Jorge Luis. "The House of Asterion." *Labyrinths: Selected Stories and Other Writings*. New York: New Directions. 1964. Print.

———. "Parable of Cervantes and the Quixote." *Collected Fictions: Volume 3*. New York: Penguin, Random House. 1998. Print.

Coupe, Laurence. *Myth*. London: Routledge. 1997. Print.

Knapp, Bettina L. *Anaïs Nin*. New York: Frederick Ungar Publishing. 1978. Print.

Nalbantian, Suzanne. *Memory in Literature: From Rousseau to Neuroscience*. Basingstoke: Palgrave Macmillan. 2003. Print.

Nin, Anaïs. *Seduction of the Minotaur*. Athens: Ohio UP. 1961. Print.

———. *The Novel of the Future*. New York: Collier Books. 1968. Print.

———. *The Diary of Anaïs Nin Volume Five (1947–1955)*. New York: Harvest. 1969. Print.

Paris, Ginette. *Pagan Meditations: Aphrodite, Hestia, Artemis*. Dallas: Spring Publications. 1986. Print.

———. *Pagan Grace: Dionysos, Hermes, and Goddess Memory in Daily Life*. Putnam: Spring Publications. 1990. Print.

Rowland, Susan. *The Ecocritical Psyche: Literature, Evolutionary Complexity and Jung*. New York: Routledge. 2012. Print.

Warner, Marina. "Boys Will be Boys." *Six Myths of Our Time*. New York: Vintage. 1994. Print.

Ziolkowski, Theodore. *Minos and the Moderns: Cretan Myth in Twentieth Century Literature and Art*. New York. Oxford UP. 2008. Print.

Epilogue

Tending self and nature: eco-minded writing and *communitas*

> In all cultural ecosystems, creativity is an important element, even though the modes and degrees of creativity are quite distinct in different fields. What seems clear, however, is that art and literature constitute a cultural ecosystem in which creativity is given a special place.
>
> (Hubert Zapf 2016)

Both her feminine subjectivity and extensive time frame (ranging from 1914 to 1974) make the work of Anaïs Nin an important example of an exploration of the depth and range of the ecology of the feminine self. Nin's works were committed to a creative process inclusive of psyche, the body and aesthetics derived from nature. Nin postulated an ecological vision; her work included details from her personal life, linked to decades of creative and personal wandering. A critical question that we face as literary critics, professors, readers and citizens is: in a prevailing ethos that fosters the inherent separation of humankind from self, each other and nature, how is eco-minded writing a tool to bridge community as we learn to better live on this planet?

A significant crisis of our time is responding to the threat of the potential catastrophic effect of our lost sense of reciprocity with nature. In this epilogue, I explore how Nin's work could help us to reframe the conflict of our age. It is my contention that Nin's views on creativity, language and the body reveal insights to a sensitivity that embraces earth-mother consciousness to help bring balance amidst writing. For Nin, writing, which has its roots in life itself, can be experienced and translated through metaphors, myths, and language into poetics, animated from the body. Mythopoesis, in this view, then, is a way to better understand inner ecologies and to see ourselves as part of an eco-field rather than split off from it.

Nature, literature and language

Throughout her life, Nin was keenly aware that the technological and scientific advances of her era presented new and difficult challenges. In the late 1960s when writing *The Novel of the Future*, Nin shared her understanding of the deep need for the people of her era to move beyond "old notions about science," leading to her urgent call for "a new synthesis" of self in literature. This "new synthesis" included "fluctuations, oscillations, and reactions. It is a matter of reassembling the fragments in a more dynamic living structure" (194–195). Nin called for a new paradigm, and the nature metaphor of the new "dynamic living structure" resonates with the concept of literature as energy that flows as a part of the physical, cultural and natural biosphere. Creativity, for Nin, is expressed through nature metaphors, as she cautions the artist against becoming a mere "map maker tracing roads already in existence" (192). Thus, for Nin, it is by perceiving experiences within a greater human landscape, not favoring consumption of landscape, and by being inclusive of the "living structure," in the living moment, that one could imagine diary writing as a part of a collective community that includes non-human nature. In addition, Nin continually valued the connection between narrative and life when creating a sense of place in her world. In her diaries, Nin records her perpetual proclivity for naming, and exploring her experiences as a way to establish a sense of self in her environment. Nin writes, "it was only when I wrote my first book that the world I wanted to live in opened to me" (1:185). By relying on myth, metaphors, and an embodied language, Nin writes herself a home.

In her diary, Nin records experiencing a certain vitality in the present and living moment of engaging mystery and connectivity, the eco-minded aspects of diary writing. She reflects:

> The power of the diary to re-create the emotional intensity of the relationship I describe makes it so potent that while I am copying it I am reliving them and seeking to understand the mysteries, the mystifying qualities of relationships altogether, when one sees the panorama, the opening (which often contains a warning one does not heed), the living core, the disintegration.
>
> (6:85)

Nin's call to engage a creative imagination that is linked to mystery, conveyed through nature metaphors and embodying the principle of connectivity to the "living core" of all things, is not limited to romantic concepts of art, but echoes the concerns of ecocritics, which I turn to next.

When considering the relationship between literature, the physical environment and its significance in literary studies, the term "ecocriticism" was first posited by William Rueckert in 1978. In his essay, "Literature and Ecology: An Experiment in Ecocriticism," he argues "human culture is connected to the physical world, affecting it and affected by it" (xix). Rueckert emphasizes the first Law of Ecology, wherein: "Everything is connected to everything else" (108). Rueckert's ecological concepts and how they relate to nature and literature are worth noting:

> A Poem is stored energy, a formal turbulence, a living thing, a swirl in the flow.
> Poems are part of the energy pathways which sustain life.

> Poems are a verbal equivalent of fossil fuel (stored energy), but they are a renewable source of energy, coming, as they do, from those ever generative twin matrices, language and imagination.
>
> (108)

Rueckert's notion of ecocriticism contests the idea that literature is a separate entity from non-human nature. Instead, ecocriticism posits that literary works derive from the creative imagination and thus contain as well as release an energy and power that is a part of a human and non-human community. It is this energy field that Nin saw as significant to creativity in her proposed "new synthesis." Also, Cheryll Glotfelty observes in the introduction of *The Ecocriticism Reader* that the focus of the definition of "ecocriticism" includes the study of interconnectedness between nature and cultural artifacts of language and literature (xix). This means that from a critical stance, ecocriticism has "one foot in literature and the other on land; as a theoretical discourse, it negotiates between the human and the nonhuman" (xix).

Susan Rowland further explores the contribution of depth psychology to the theories binding nature, literature, the human mind and somatic experience with language. In her book *The Ecocritical Psyche: Literature, Evolutionary Complexity and Jung* (2012), Rowland points out that the creative nature of humanity has a substantive link between the human mind and non-human nature. Expounding on the bridge between language, the imagination and the body, Rowland underscores that writing and images have the capacity to conjure "the deep unconscious," which embeds human nature in non-human nature (Rowland 20). The human unconscious is a part of nature and intrinsically creative; hence, the psyche has an inherent ecocritical perspective. To develop her argument, Rowland notes that since Jung's conceptual model of the unconscious is seen as a segment of "evolved nature, with archetypes functioning as part of the natural order" it follows that "language has a fundamental root in non-human nature" (Rowland 20). Rowland's argument, underscoring Jung's proposal that language is rooted in the body, expands our understanding of literature and ecology. By drawing on Jung's important suggestion, "that the unconscious is intrinsically creative and partly unknowable, indicates a different emphasis to both ego formation and the relationship with language" (Rowland 20). By linking human subjectivity as involved with the "highly skilled unconscious," Jung sees creativity as a legacy from the womb (Rowland 20). This was a way for Jung to "de-throne the phallus" (Rowland 20). Elevating the feminine principle, and ways of being in the world, was a way for Jung to underscore another creation myth in Western consciousness. Nin, like Jung, sought to debunk the fallacy of single-sided, logo-centric thinking, in efforts to invite the conjunction of myriad ways of knowing. While responding to the androcentric dualism between men/women at the time was important to Nin, she does not suggest a mere gender essentialist approach, as I have posited in my analysis in Chapters 2 and 3. Rather, Nin instead resorts to a philosophical orientation that includes an eco-sensitivity. It is within her use of myth, metaphor and language that Nin critiques a society that privileged the masculine gender and constructs a credo rooted in earth-mother consciousness. However, by writing about the personal while planted in the womb – not the womb as an exclusively feminine organ, but the womb as a source of creativity and earth-mother consciousness – Nin infuses her work with the presence, strength and order of sky-father consciousness, conjuring a connection to a "collective emotional identity" (*A Woman Speaks* 163).

Later in her life, Nin credited her ardent passion and respect of diary writing for bestowing her with the interest and capacity to nurture an emotional topography that was key to deepening her understanding of the archetypal nature of her experiences. It is this emotional engagement with diary writing that Nin remarks on when she states:

> An immediate, emotional reaction to experience reveals that the power to re-create lies in the sensibilities rather than intellectual memory or observation. This personal reaction I found to be the core of individuality, or originality and personality. A deep personal relation to all things reaches far beyond the personal into the general.
>
> (*The Novel of the Future* 159)

In this passage, Nin reminds us that "the sensibilities" of the personal voice provide a glimpse into our vulnerable and emotional lives. If one is willing to risk the personal, it is possible to reach "beyond," to explore perspectives and interconnections necessary to build sustainable communities.

In 1972, Nin attributes a dream with vivifying her vision of the vital interconnection between writing, life, death and the subterranean energy field transforming narratives. In the dream, Nin is physically in a garden and her hair sprouts out of her skull as she carefully writes words on it. She proceeds to make a braid out of her hair, and as the braid grows longer, she tosses it over "the high wall of [her] garden" (*A Woman Speaks* 225). Here there is a spirited link between the human subject and a symbolic life force that is linked to nature. The dream captures an encounter with the mystery of nature, in its interfusion of metaphor and narrative of isolation and communication, visible and invisible, life and death. It is this process of a creative engagement with her body, life forces, including the environment, that Nin credits with allowing her to find the "way out" of a once-isolated life. Reflecting on the dream, she writes, "[n]ow this was a dream, and the reality was that the first book I wrote then connected me with the vivacious literary life of Paris. It was the writing which was the way out" (*A Woman Speaks* 225).

Privatizing nature and food

A recent example of the relationship in humankind's misplaced reciprocity with nature is evidenced in the developing relationship between the industrialization of food and patenting of parts of nature. A brief look at Monsanto's genetic modification of food reveals not only a de-mythologizing of food creation, but also a detachment from our animistic connection to nourishment, and thus to elements of the natural world.

A close consideration of the myth of modernity, i.e., the Judeo-Christian creation myth, illuminates, from a mythological perspective, the rise of the corporate manipulation of the agricultural order. This origin myth is the dominant paradigm of consciousness with respect to the natural world. In Genesis, God tells man: "Be fertile and increase, fill the earth and master it; and rule the fish of the sea, the birds of the sky, and all the living things that creep on earth. I have given you every herb that yields seed which is on the face of all the earth, and every tree whose fruit yields seed; to you it shall be for food" (*Holy Bible*, 1:28). This myth implies not only that woman is invisible, but underscores too that man is "above" and has power over nature, for nature exists separate from man. The conviction of man's superiority over nature is captured in a phrase Scott Pruitt, Administrator of the U.S. Environmental Protection Agency, uttered before Congress: "We have been blessed, as a country, with tremendous natural resources." When asked to define his phrase "true environmentalism," he notes, "[it is] using resources that God has blessed us with to feed the world" (Pereira).

This "over-valuing" of sky-father transcendence as the dominant attitude in the world leads to the modern consideration of man as superior to nature, and therefore, in the position to control his creation. As a result, "the 'logos,' the abstract knowledge of the natural world, ceased to be identified primarily with the mind of God and became the dominant (and privileged) mode of knowledge as science" (Rowland 287). The emphasis on scientific logos, in the guise of modern technology, can be observed in the genetic modification of our foods today, specifically with regard to the industrial processes of one of the world's leading chemical companies, Monsanto (formerly known as Aroclor, famed manufacturer of the carcinogenic fluid polychlorinated biphenyl [PCB]) (Robin 3).

Marie-Monique Robin in *The World According to Monsanto: Pollution, Corruption, and the Control of Our Food Supply*, traces the company's history with their own brand of synthesizing in the laboratory as they prepared to modify the DNA of certain foods. Robin notes that Monsanto began by manufacturing saccharin, the first artificial sweetener, and in "1918 Monsanto made its first acquisition, buying an Illinois company that made sulfuric acid" (Robin 11). Monsanto's history reveals an inclination for artificial creation:

> In the 1940s it became one of the world's major producers of rubber, followed by plastics and synthetic fibers such as polystyrene, as well as phosphates . . . At the same time, it reinforced its monopoly in the international market of PCB market, guaranteed by a patent that enabled it to sell licenses almost everywhere in the world.
>
> (11)

While it is unclear whether Nin had knowledge of these specific Monsanto developments during her time, it is evident that the possibility of corporate monopoly and the likelihood of relying on a mechanistic world view were known to her. Nin speaks to the importance of using writing as a way to orient self within a world believing in the mechanization of nature. She writes the following of her diary:

> Not as a work of literature, but as something necessary to living, as a way of orienting ourselves to our inner lives. It doesn't matter in what form you do it, whether it's meditation, whether it's writing or whether it's just a moment of thoughtfulness about the trend, the current, of your life. It's a moment of stopping life in order to become aware of it. And it's this kind of awareness which is threatened in our world today, with its acceleration and with its mechanization.
>
> (*A Woman Speaks* 160)

The "mechanization" that Nin references above, is exemplified in the genesis of genetic modifications of foods, which according to Robin, began in 1953, when biochemist James Watson and Francis Crick "discovered the double helix structure of DNA (deoxyribonucleic acid), the molecule that contains the genetic code for every living organism" (132). In 1972 Monsanto began working on developing seeds that would be resistant to their leading pesticide, Roundup, by altering the DNA of their seeds. Today Monsanto has the patent on 11,000 specific seeds, including many of the world's staple crops, including corn, soy and canola. Monsanto also holds a patent on a variety of wheat used for making traditional Indian foods such as *chapattis* (Robin 293). Monsanto epitomizes the modern paradigm dominated by patriarchy and Judeo-Christian ethos, resulting in a gross devaluing of nature's logic including the instinctive yield that was once produced by nature alone. The biotechnology Monsanto uses to produce food is blatantly devoid of a mythic sensitivity towards food formation, bereft of the manual skill and labor knowledge that is essential not only for vibrant and diverse economies, but for our association as gatherers with an inveterate connection to the natural world. The increasing impoverishment of nature's logic leads to our detachment from the intimate relationship with food.

By removing the ancestral connection between humankind, nature and food, Vandana Shiva, in her outstanding book *Soil Not Oil*, cautions us that as industrial agriculture grows, so too do fossil fuel economies greatly substituting energy for humans. It is these processes that have rendered humans redundant to the economic enterprise of food production (138). Shiva argues that "human energy, combined with the energy of the sun, the plants and animals, the wind, the air, the sea and water, the soil and the earth, is both the basis of work and livelihoods and the source of sustainable and renewable energy" (139). This "energy" is reminiscent of Rueckert's notion of the interconnected relationship stored in poetics in relation to the environment. However, in our current mechanistic worldview, the word "energy" has lost its original meaning as a life-giving element. Energy, Shiva notes, is not measured in British thermal units, but rather means

Shakti: "the generative force of the universe, to the sun that powers our lives, to the water that comes to us as bountiful rain or a flood or a tsunami, to the air and the wind that move the clouds and create the climate. Energy is not just oil and gas. Energy is an all-pervasive element of life" (134–135). The industrialization of food, in its detachment from a knowledge base that includes wisdom and skill of "energy," and human labor, represents a regression in our world.

An essential metaphor missing from the Christian creation myth, yet by contrast prominent in Iroquois mythology, as noted in Chapter 2, is the power attributed to the birthing of life from the Earth, as the source of abundance. This myth reveals that the connection between nature's truest cycle (life, death and rebirth), food and the body, goes back millennia. In the Seneca creation myth, for example, Sky Woman's daughter dies during the birthing of twins, and her son Good Mind watches as crops sprout from his mother's life-transforming body:

> Good Mind watched at the grave of his mother and watered the earth above it until the grass grew. He continued to watch until he saw strange buds coming out of the ground. Where the feet were the earth sprouted with a plant that became the stringed-potato, where her fingers lay sprang the beans, where her abdomen lay sprang the squash, where her breasts lay sprang the corn plant, and from the spot above her forehead sprang the tobacco plant.
>
> (Parker 64)

This creation myth maintains earth at the core of all that pertains to flourishing foods, as the "three sisters" (corn, beans and squash) become the revered and main life support that feeds and nourishes society. In the Iroquois community women are known to be the farmers, passing down ancestral knowledge about the specific agricultural methods. The image of vegetables sprouting from the body of Sky Woman's daughter echoes Nin's dream of words growing from her hair. This is an image that unites Nin to her own creative awakening, to a deeper self through the voice of the earth. As stated in Chapter 2, Nin's diaries contain a record of the seeds awakening toward somatic consciousness. This is a way to gain an intimate "humanism," which sustains life as a part of a greater ecosystem.

Paths of possibility: language, dynamic living and risk

Nin's diaries reveal a process of creating a sense of self and place in the cosmos by pursuing her own life flow. It was Nin's contention that writing invites us to take risks as we learn to pay dynamic attention to our inner world while better understanding our known stance in the grander world. We still live in a "culture [that] has a suspicion of what people do when they turn inward" (*A Woman Speaks* 156). Our culture also distrusts speaking about nature and the female body for fear of essentializing a feminine experience. Nin's works show us that earth-mother consciousness helps weave a narrative that embodies an alternative potential that is an act of respect to self and one's sense of place in the greater landscape. Through eco-minded writing we recognize life as a sacred transaction, and come to know it as a form of mystery connected to a greater living organism, including non-human nature.

Nin's contributions to eco-minded writing can be seen in her lifelong efforts to orient her sense of self through her poetic writing. For Nin, the writer need not be constrained by imposed models, but pursue that which is natural to psyche, nature and self. Conversely, Nin's diaries demonstrate that when we dare to disclose our innermost thoughts, at the risk of sounding biased and subjective, we call the indigenous voices back to our bodies. Nin asserts that through the capacity to reflect and listen to the sounds, mysteries and currents of one's life, literature could pay heed to all voices in our communities, including non-human nature. This receptivity, according to Nin, cultivates a continuum of integrity between the feminine and masculine principles, rather than merely disembodied, logos-centered knowing. Eco-minded writing opens the "secret chambers" that link a longing to name, to better understand the past and present, including the human and the non-human mysteries (7:199). By creating stories that reflect our humanity, inspire and awaken Eros for all species, we could better buttress communities that struggle for personal growth and *communitas*.

Works cited

Glotfelty, Cheryll. "Introduction: Literary Studies in an Age of Environmental Crisis." *The Ecocriticsm Reader*. Eds. Cheryll Glotfelty and Harold Fromm. London: The U of Georgia P. 1996. Print.

Hinz, Evelyn J. Ed. *A Woman Speaks: The Lectures, Seminars, and Interviews of Anaïs Nin*. Chicago: Swallow Press. 1975. Print.

Holy Bible: *The New King James Version*. New York: ABS. 1982. Print.

Nin, Anaïs. *The Novel of the Future*. New York: Collier Books. 1968. Print.

———. *The Diary of Anaïs Nin Volume One (1931–1934)*. New York: Harvest. 1969a. Print.

———. *The Diary of Anaïs Nin Volume Six (1955–1966)*. New York: Harvest. 1969c. Print.

———. *The Diary of Anaïs Nin Volume Seven (1966–1974)*. New York: Harvest. 1969d. Print.

Parker, Arthur C. *Seneca Myths and Folk Tales*. Lincoln: Nebraska UP. 1923. Print.

Pereira, Sidney. "What Is 'True Environmentalism'? Here's What Trump's EPA Had to Say." December 29, 2017. *Newsweek*. www.newsweek.com/epa-admin-scott-pruitt-thinks-using-fossil-fuels-true-environmentalism-760265.

Robin, Marie-Monique. *The World According to Monsanto: Pollution, Corruption, and the Control of Our Food Supply*. New York: New Press. 2008. Print.

Rowland, Susan. *The Ecocritical Psyche: Literature, Evolutionary Complexity and Jung*. New York: Routledge. 2012. Print.

Rueckert, William. "Literature and Ecology: An Experiment in Ecocriticsm." *The Ecocriticsm Reader*. Eds. Cheryll Glotfelty and Harold Fromm. London: Georgia UP. 1996. Print.

Shiva, Vandana. *Soil Not Oil*. New York: South End Press. 2008. Print.

Zapf, Hubert. *Literature as Culture Ecology*. London: Bloomsbury Academic. 2016. Print.

Index

For Product Safety Concerns and Information please contact our
EU representative GPSR@taylorandfrancis.com Taylor & Francis
Verlag GmbH, Kaufingerstraße 24, 80331 München, Germany